"[*A Parent's Guide* is] indispensable for parents sending their first (or second or third) child off to college. [Joel Epstein offers] straight talk for parents who think that the college experience is as it was twenty or thirty years ago. I wish we had this book when our son went off to college; we'd have been a lot less naïve."
—Stephen Clem, Executive Director, Association of Independent Schools in New England

"This is a well-informed guide to life at college as it is now being lived. Joel Epstein handles the 'hot button' issues in a mature, measured, and thoughtful manner. Any parent of a college student should find this book a helpful and useful resource."
—Stephen Singer, Director of College Counseling, Horace Mann School

"*A Parent's Guide to Sex, Drugs, and Flunking Out* provides readers with a no-holds-barred look at the current undergraduate experience at many of America's colleges and universities. The book tackles the very subjects that many parents would like to ignore or, at the very least, deny apply to their child. Epstein's realistic and straightforward approach to such sensitive subjects may provide parents with many sleepless nights but will certainly help them better understand the many obstacles and challenges that their children will face in college and in adolescent life in today's world."
—Mary Stuart Hunter, Director, National Resource Center for the First-Year Experience and Students in Transition

"*A Parent's Guide to Sex, Drugs, and Flunking Out* should be required reading for parents of college students, college-bound students, guidance counselors, and anyone else who wants to be well informed about the multiple issues that affect the college years. Joel Epstein uses his extensive knowledge, wisdom, and humor as he provides answers and information. This book is an invaluable, up-to-date resource."
—Judith C. Hochman, Director, Windward Teacher Training Institute, and former Head of School, Windward School, White Plains, New York

"*A Parent's Guide* delivers authoritative advice in a relaxed and good humored manner. As a resource for parents, it is well researched and sensibly arranged, with dozens of Web site suggestions providing a timely edge. I found it refreshingly frank about such matters as alcohol and drug use, sexuality, and campus security, and I recommend it to anyone with college-bound kids."
—**Gregory Gibson, Author of** *Goneboy: A Walkabout*

"Joel Epstein has penned an invaluable resource guide on student wellness and campus safety. [This book is] must reading for prospective college students and their parents."
—**Rayburn Barton, Executive Director, South Carolina Commission on Higher Education**

"The college years can be the best or worst of times for young people off on their own for the first time. Parents are right to worry: How do I help my children select the right school? How do I help them prepare to take on more responsibility for their own care and well-being? How do I stay in touch without being overbearing? Joel Epstein has done a superb job of outlining the major issues that parents need to think and ask about as their children prepare to go off to college, and he offers a wealth of information and resources that will help ease the transition. Even if your child is only a high school freshman, it's not too soon to buy and use this book."
—**William DeJong, Professor, Boston University School of Public Health, and Director, Higher Education Center for Alcohol and Other Drug Prevention**

"Sending a son or daughter off to college is a formidable task, especially for parents who do not have 'inside' information. Joel Epstein exposes parents to a plethora of issues that they will face through their children."
—**Peter Lake, Professor of Law, Stetson University**

A PARENT'S GUIDE TO

SEX, DRUGS AND FLUNKING OUT

**Answers
to the Questions
Your College Student
Doesn't Want You
to Ask**

JOEL EPSTEIN

◪ HAZELDEN®

VIRGINIA BEACH PUBLIC LIBRARY SYSTEM
4100 Virginia Beach Boulevard 23452-1767

VA BEACH PUBLIC LIBRARY SYSTEM-DUP

A18230   286936

Hazelden
Center City, Minnesota 55012-0176

1-800-328-0094
1-651-213-4590 (Fax)
www.hazelden.org

©2001 by Joel C. Epstein
All rights reserved. Published 2001
Printed in the United States of America
No portion of this publication may be reproduced in any manner
without the written permission of the publisher

Library of Congress Cataloging-in-Publication Data

Epstein, Joel.
    A parents guide to sex, drugs, and flunking out : answers to the ques-
tions your college student doesn't want you to ask / Joel C. Epstein.
        p. cm.
    Includes bibliographical references and index.
    ISBN 1-56838-571-4 (pbk.)
    1. Education, Higher—Parent participation—United States. 2. College
choice—United States. 3. College students—United States.

    LB2350.5 .E68 2001
    378.1'98—dc21

                                                            2001024800

05   04   03   02   01   6   5   4   3   2

Cover design by Theresa Gedig
Interior design by Elizabeth Cleveland
Typesetting by Stanton Publication Services, Inc.

Contents

Acknowledgments

This book would not have been possible without the generous support and encouragement of Karen Sarachik and our children Gabe, Julia, and Clara. It is dedicated to them. I am also grateful to my parents, in-laws, sisters, and brothers-in-law for their thoughtful and helpful suggestions regarding various drafts and topics for the book. Special thanks go to Cathy Kirshner who read every word and performed much-needed expert surgery on an early draft. Her careful reading, editing, and thoughtful criticism helped make the book far more interesting, useful, and reader-friendly than it would otherwise have been. Similarly, essential to the collaborative process of writing this book was Bette Nowacki, my editor at Hazelden. Bette's comments, encouragement, and, of course, thousands of edits, large and small, helped me find my literary voice and keep the book on track. Thanks are due as well to Kris Vanhoof-Haines, who recognized the need for the book and took a chance on me as its author, and Tracy Snyder, my manuscript editor. Lastly, I owe much thanks to the many experts, parents, and students who gave so generously of their time in helping me think through the goals of the book and to the staff of the Health and Human Development Programs division at the Education Development Center. At the risk of leaving someone out, I wish to thank in particular Jonathan Benjamin, Jon Bertman, Bob Bickel, Kenny Breuer, Tim Brooks, S. Daniel Carter, Howard Clery, Rosella Bonilla Coronado, Bill DeJong, Stanley Epstein, Sylvia H. Epstein, Janelle Farris, Richard M. Flaherty, Belle Frank, Jane Frantz,

Anne Foster, Wes Gardenswartz, Theodore Geisel, Michelle Goldfarb, Laura Gomberg, Deborah Hahn, Steve Healy, Steve Hedrick, Bradley M. Henry, Deborah Epstein Henry, Gordon M. Henry, Rand Hutcheson, Stephanie Ives, Heather Karjane, John Katzman, Thomas King, Jon Kirshner, Mary Kocol, Andrew Kuhn, Peter Lake, Jeffrey Levy, Karl Lindholm, Elizabeth Marks, Pat McCoy, Mothers Against Drunk Driving, Meg Muckenhoupt, Siobhan Murphy, Gary Rhodes, Bob Rollins, Adam Rosen, Barbara Rosen, Julia E. Rosenbaum, Eric Rubin, Miles A. Rubin, Susie Rubin, Benjamin Samuels, Matthew S. Santirocco, Holly Sateia, Diane Schulman, Jeffrey M. Sherman, Josh Slater, Brett Sokolow, Helen Stubbs, Amy Vogt, Steven M. Ward, Cheryl Vince Whitman, Kit Williams, Dan Wohlfeiler, Diana Zimmerman, and Karen Zweig. Their input and comments, many of which are incorporated verbatim with attribution into the text, have immeasurably enhanced the final product.

Introduction

"The road to hell is paved with good intentions." As a teenager and well into my twenties, I felt haunted by this adage—my mother's favorite. It wasn't until I had my own children that my mother's words rang true for me. Perhaps this is how many college-bound young men or women see their parents' attempts to help with the sometimes difficult decisions regarding college life.

Dr. Tim Brooks, the former dean of students at the University of Delaware, who saw two sons off to college recently, notes, "Separation anxiety is something we all have when our children go off to school. The trick is to be supportive without interfering. Chances are your son or daughter will do extremely well without you looking over his or her shoulder."[1] Even if parents want to have more influence in the lives of their children, once the kids leave for school, parents' influence is largely diminished.

Parents need to learn to let go; they can hem and haw all they like, but their children are still going to stay up too late and make other ill-advised decisions once they are away at school. Jon Kirshner, a Great Neck, New York, father of a Harvard senior and a Syracuse freshman, recalls how, after a few months of nagging his then-freshman daughter over the phone and e-mail to go to bed earlier, she informed him as gently as she could, "Daddy, I'm here and you're there. You can't do anything about it."[2]

"In many cases, our children are electing to attend colleges and universities tens of miles, perhaps thousands of miles from our homes," notes John Gardner, executive director of the Policy Center on the First Year of College and a distinguished professor of educational leadership at Brevard College in North Carolina.[3] In an interview in the spring 2000 issue of *Prevention File,* Dr. Gardner explains that parents have far more influence over the high school their child attends through their community and local school board than they do over the college their son or daughter selects.[4]

Going to a local college, of course, has its advantages. My parents attended Brooklyn College, a short ride on the subway from their families' apartments. In those days, Brooklyn College was a diamond in the rough, equal in quality, if not prestige, to the famed City College, the former jewel in the crown of New York City's public university system. Brooklyn College, like the public high schools my parents had attended before it, was a place to soak up as much as you could before heading off on your own to pursue the American dream. Both my parents lived at home during their college years. Their separation from family came later, for my father when he attended medical school in Chicago and for my mother when my parents married and moved to California, where my father did his postgraduate training and my mother completed graduate school. As it was for so many immigrants and their American-born children, education was my parents' ticket out of their childhood neighborhoods, and God forbid their children should ever forget that it was free public higher education at that.

Like the diverse collection of parents reading this book, my parents were themselves the products of different views on higher education. My mother's parents, both New York City schoolteachers, had five undergraduate and graduate degrees between them and held a college education in the highest regard. Though somewhat important to my father's parents, higher education for them was something you pursued so far as you needed it to earn your keep. Thankfully for my father, he lived in New York, an American city, then nearly unique in its recognition of the role of local government in fostering public higher education.

Ironically, as strong as my parents' commitment to public education was, they chose for me, their eldest child, a private college preparatory school. Disappointed with the education I was receiving in a generally well-regarded suburban public school in Westchester County, New York, they chose for me a selective private school some thirty minutes from our home. For six years, beginning in sixth grade, I commuted to this ivy-covered cloister on a hill, a perfectly beautiful setting and one that I detest to this day.

Perhaps it was my failure as a teenager to communicate my utter distaste for my private high school that inspired me to write this book. At its core, this book is about communication between parents and their children. While no guarantee of success, keeping open the lines of communication with your child will increase the probability that your child chooses the right school for him- or herself and makes the most of the college experience.

The years seem to have flown by. With college visits on the horizon or having already begun, you may be wondering whether you have adequately cherished the time with your child. How well do you know your child? Have you stayed close or gotten reacquainted these past few years, or are you anticipating that the chance to travel together to look at schools will be that long-awaited opportunity to reconnect? Did you get to know him or her before the time came to start looking at colleges? Do you think you know what is best for your child, both now and for the future? Are you prepared to let go, and, if so, in what ways?

Though I am writing this book for parents of college-bound children, perhaps the best time to read it is when your children are still young, respectful, and impressed with your achievements and authority. A cynical but widely expressed remark I have heard from dozens of parents is, "It's too late by the time they are off to college." Well, since you have already bought the book, you might as well read on. And when you are done, please pass the book on, or better yet, buy another copy for your friends and family members who have young children.

ONE

The Right School for Your Child— And You

◪ ◪ ◪

ONE OF THE FIRST TOUGH DECISIONS

For most young people who are graduating from high school, selecting the right college is one of the toughest decisions they will have had to make. While parents play a role in helping a child select the right school, ultimately it is the child who must select the school. In this time of relative economic prosperity in the United States, college-bound sons and daughters may be less mindful than earlier generations of the need to pick a college that will put them on the road to a promising career. Our role, then, as parents is to unobtrusively help our children find a school that will be right for the future, not just for the New York–minute economy that the Internet seemed for a while to have spawned.

Parents can also help their child by accepting that, for some, college is not the best place to be the moment they reach that magical age at which most sons and daughters complete high school. Some students at seventeen, eighteen, or nineteen are not ready to go to college. These teens might be better off deferring their start date, entering the workforce for a year or more, or staying in high school for a so-called "thirteenth year."

Many private schools offer thirteenth-year programs to help prepare high school graduates who are not quite ready for college.

Students who missed out on the basics in high school or never learned how to study and students who have disabilities that require different approaches to learning may find these programs invaluable to their college experience. Although tuition costs for such programs can be steep, so can the cost of a wasted year of college.

In later life, people who took a year off between high school and college often acknowledge that their having taken the time to think things through before heading off to college was the best thing they ever did. Others recognize that they needed that added year to improve study habits or finish the college preparatory work they did not complete prior to graduation from high school. For those parents who do not think their child made much of the extra year, they need to compare that year with the time that might have been lost had their child gone on to college unprepared. Would the teen have flunked classes, dropped out, or wasted a year's worth of tuition on beer?

Parents and students who come to the difficult realization that a student may not be ready just yet to go on to college will later find the college experience much more meaningful and beneficial to the student. How and why we mature to a point where we can make the most of higher education is the subject for another day and another book. The important lesson is that it is no disgrace to wait until ready to attend college.

AN AMERICAN COLLEGE PROFILE

Parents should encourage their children to make the choice of a college conscientiously. Not everyone has the luxury of going to college. On a recent trip to Los Angeles I met a young man who is simply happy to be alive and holding down a modest job. This heavily scarred and tattooed former gang member may go to college someday, but for now his hopes and dreams are tied to a nine-to-five job at HomeBoy Industries, a gang prevention microenterprise program in

East Los Angeles. Unlike most college-bound children, this survivor came by his higher education *grâce à* the California Youth Authority. Instead of fight songs and college cheers, he lives by the wisdom, "I'd rather be judged by twelve, than carried [to my grave] by six."

Not everyone goes to college, but many do. According to the Washington, D.C.–based National Center for Education Statistics, in 2000, over 15.1 million students were enrolled in colleges and universities in the United States with enrollment in colleges and graduate schools to grow to 17.5 million by 2010.[1] These students are spread out over the country's 3,500 public and private colleges and universities. In his 1994 book *American Higher Education,* Christopher J. Lucas has described the nation's schools as the following:

> an untidy array of small liberal arts colleges, two-year community colleges, technical institutes, local and regional universities, and sprawling research universities, both public and private, with different but overlapping identities, missions, and functions.[2]

While most colleges and universities in the United States tend to be either public or private nonprofit, a recent trend noted by the National Center for Education Statistics is the growth of private, for-profit universities. As of 1998, there were 669 such institutions, a development that may reflect a general trend toward introducing competitive business practices into the "ivory tower."[3] A higher education consumer rights movement began to emerge in the early 1990s and has been gaining strength ever since. Calls for accountability by students and parents continue to send shivers up the backs of college administrators who, as a group, have never before been challenged on their academic leadership and vision. With tuition and expenses at many private colleges exceeding $35,000 per year since the late 1990s, perhaps it is time that consumer advocates took aim at American higher education with the same spirit with which they have long been confronting Detroit and the U.S. automobile industry.

TOWARD A MORE DIVERSE COLLEGE CLASS

With the U.S. college student population growing and becoming as increasingly diverse as the colleges themselves, the selection process—on the part of both students and admissions officers—has become increasingly difficult. According to Steven M. Ward, chief of the Department of Public Safety at the University of Southern California, which is located in Los Angeles, the most diverse American city,

- more than half of all U.S. students are women
- an estimated 45 percent are over the age of twenty-five
- nearly a quarter of all students are from an ethnic or racial minority[4]

According to a 2000 study by the Educational Testing Service, college enrollment in the United States is expected to increase four million to nineteen million by 2015 with African American, Latino, and Asian American students accounting for 80 percent of the growth. Whereas in 1995, 71 percent of all college students reported their race as white, in 2015 that proportion of white students on campuses nationally is projected to be 63 percent. A small handful of states—Arizona, California, Florida, New York, and Texas—will account for over half of the overall growth in the undergraduate population.[5]

The data is not as straightforward as it might seem, however. Some observers express concern that the study may lead to the erroneous conclusion that the country has achieved its diversity goals. While white college enrollment continues to increase dramatically, it simply is not growing as fast as the age eighteen to twenty-four African American and Latino populations. According to the Educational Testing Service, enrollment by African Americans and Latinos in higher education will actually decrease in proportion to their populations between 1995 and 2015.[6]

With groups like the American Council on Education (ACE) committed to racial and ethnic diversity in higher education, efforts continue to diversify college student bodies and faculties. The goal is to try to make colleges and universities more comfortable places for students who have been historically underrepresented.

In an effort to diversify and to make formerly underrepresented students feel at home, many schools focus on topics of tolerance and diversity during first-year student orientation programs, confronting prejudice at the outset of a student's college career. In my view, promoting tolerance and diversity are the goals most essential to the maintenance of racial, ethnic, cultural, and social harmony on campus. To the credit of the nation's colleges and in recognition of demographic realities, the racial and ethnic diversification of American higher education can be expected to continue for years to come.

ALL THINGS TO ALL PEOPLE

Exactly what your son or daughter wants and needs in a school is what many colleges are striving to be. As major American businesses, colleges' livelihood depends on convincing students and parents that their campus is *the* place to go to school. Colleges market and sell themselves to us just as any other product or service industry sells itself. One look through the magazines in the racks in September when *U.S. News and World Report* and *Time* come out with their college issues tells it all.

There is considerable variety in the market, and not all "education" is created equal. For the scholar or privileged few, university life continues to take place in ivy-covered quadrangles in Cambridge, New Haven, or Palo Alto—at undergraduate universities renown for their scholarship and commitment to Learning. For others, college is a large land grant school—one of the Midwest's Big Ten schools with football, marching bands, and a widely diverse student population. Between and alongside, the lot is as different from one another and from the Big Ten as they come—MIT, Grinnell, Miami, Carleton, Oberlin, USC, the University of California,

Lafayette, Colgate, Williams, Hampshire, and Wellesley, to name just a few. Add to these the many public and private historically black colleges and universities, the Native American tribal colleges, the junior and community colleges, and the firmly religiously affiliated schools like Boston College, Notre Dame, Yeshiva University, and Southern Methodist. With all of the choices available, how can parents help their children select the school that is best for them?

IT'S YOUR CHILD'S SCHOOL, NOT YOURS

Consider Personality

Parents can help their college-bound student find the right school, with the right sort of social environment, by helping their son or daughter think through what sort of person he or she really is. For example, a shy student with strong grades might want to resist the temptation to apply to a large, highly competitive university known for chewing up and spitting out its undergraduates. As obvious as that seems, too many students ignore such advice and end up at colleges that anyone can see are wrong for them.

Parents, too, may need to turn off *their* own desires to see their child attend that ever-so-highly thought of university, when it really is not the place the student should be. Ask yourself on behalf of your child, and have your son or daughter ask him- or herself, "In what sort of environment do I thrive? Will I feel comfortable at this school? Will I have the courage to speak up in class and to attend campus social events?" If the answers are, "No, but it's such a fine school it will serve me to have gone there," then have the courage and the wisdom to support your child in a decision to look elsewhere.

The reality is, many students get through schools that are not right for them, but at what cost? Many students suffer severe depression and find themselves feeling terribly alone. Others turn to drugs and alcohol or get involved in relationships that may not be healthy, supportive ones.

Legacy

Legacy is another important issue for many students and parents facing the "Where should I go?" decision. For many students, a family alma mater is often on their short list. Accepting that the place you went to college and to whose alumni association you have been contributing all of these years may not be right for your son or daughter can be a real challenge. In addition, because of a desire to strike out on their own, some students may want to cross schools off their list that parents or siblings attended even though the schools might actually be quite right for them. Carefully consider your and your child's motivations to attend or not attend such a school with the same critical thought reserved for other top-choice schools. In other words, if the school is right for your child *and* you happened to go there, keep it under consideration. Keeping the exchange between parents and teens as candid as possible will help students avoid making choices they never would have made before their heads were clouded by a parent's wishes.

Staying Near or Going Far

Attending a college close to home is one way many college students and their families avoid many of the difficult social realities that are part of going away to college. Although Americans are by and large a highly mobile people, the research suggests that most college students choose to stay fairly close to home when it comes time to select a college. However, because many colleges want a geographically diverse student body, those willing to travel farther away to attend college may fare better gaining admission to a similarly ranked pool of colleges than those who stay closer to home. So what will it be, a school farther from home and less familiar or one nearby but harder to gain admission to because all of your son's or daughter's classmates hope to attend it as well? Perhaps the best question for students and parents then is—will the student feel alone and too far from family and friends if he or she attends a school hundreds or thousands of miles from home?

Challenges of Going Far

Small colleges located in rural or isolated communities are presented with their own challenges in appealing to students and parents. Lauren, who grew up in a Chicago suburb, is a 2000 graduate of Green Mountain College in rural Poultney, Vermont. With just 650 full-time students and little social or cultural activity available in the community, drinking at the lone bar in town or at student parties on- and off-campus is a common pastime for both legal age and underage students. Being far from home added to Lauren's challenge of being at a small rural college. In a conversation following her graduation she noted, "Most students at Green Mountain come from Vermont, New Hampshire, New York, and Connecticut. Coming from the Midwest, I was pretty unusual."[7] Speaking of the social scene and drinking and drug use at her college, Lauren adds:

> It's easy to get alcohol with a fake ID or from older students. And it's easy to get a fake ID either from a friend or over the Web. The school bans kegs in the room, but alcohol is everywhere. There's also lots of marijuana, Ecstasy, and other drugs like mushrooms and cocaine. Though there aren't any raves around Poultney, a lot of students are into Ecstasy.[8]

History of Alcohol or Other Drug Abuse

Alcoholism or a family history of alcohol or drug abuse is another consideration for many college students seeking a school that will help them achieve their maximum potential. According to 2000 data from both the Core Institute at Southern Illinois University and the National Institute on Alcohol Abuse and Alcoholism (NIAAA), one in four college students has a parent who has abused alcohol or other drugs.[9]

Other Factors to Consider

Whether your son or daughter was a wallflower or the center of attention at every high school party, college social life should be a fresh start, one that presents a variety of opportunities for students. Unlike most students' high school experiences, college life can be extremely varied, offering students real choices, such as dorm living versus off-campus housing, Greek organizations versus non-Greek activities, liberal arts–oriented majors versus pre-professional majors, and an urban environment versus a rural setting, to name a few. Factors that should enter into a student's decision about which college to attend and factors that will affect his or her social life at college include the following:

- the student's housing preference
- how well the student is prepared academically for college
- the college's focus on athletics
- the college's commitment to Greek life
- the student's involvement in extracurricular activities
- the willingness of the student to be somewhat tolerant in his or her attitude toward a roommate

Most high school students do not have the luxury of choosing which high school to attend. For many, college is another story entirely, with students able to choose between tens of different kinds of colleges and college environments. While some of the challenge of "succeeding" socially at college involves luck, picking the right school is terribly important. Picking the right school is also something your son or daughter has far more control over than he or she probably realizes.

THE COLLEGE VISIT

One of the most valuable resources available to students and parents who are choosing a college from among a number of acceptances is the college visit itself. Because of the cost of visiting colleges, many students apply without first visiting the schools. Once your child has been accepted and you're about to make what may be one of the largest investments of your life, there is simply no substitute for viewing the school firsthand.

During the campus visit, a school's geographic location or re-moteness may suddenly become a more important issue for some students. For example, a May 3, 2000, article in the *New York Times* quotes a student with admissions to several prestigious colleges who said, "Williams [in mostly rural northwestern Massachusetts] is a school that most parents and teachers think is great, simply because it's rated high academically. . . . But socially, it's out in the middle of nowhere."[10]

Although your child may not want to visit schools with you tag-ging along, you are perfectly entitled to accompany your son or daughter on campus visits, keeping in mind that it is the child and not you who will be going off to college. Look and listen to everything with a critical eye and open mind. What are the students telling you about their college experience? If you go on a Friday or over a week-end, observe the social scene. Are classes even held on Friday? What is the culture of the school, as described by the students you meet? For me, the guided college tour offers a bland but generally necessary overview. Often more useful and informative are the casual discus-sions that your son or daughter may strike up with normal students, students outside of the official admissions office greeting cadre.

At a recent college night in an affluent northern New Jersey com-munity, a student stood up and asked rhetorically, "Isn't it better to visit the schools without your parents?" To the student's surprise, the speaker, an admissions officer from Cornell, answered "no" and went on to explain that this applied unless the student was going to pay for school alone. Elaborating, the admissions officer added that parents can and should be on hand if possible to serve as critical eyes and ears willing to pose questions the student may not have thought of or been concerned with.[11]

Eliciting the right information during a campus visit can be vital to the decision-making process. The *U.S. News and World Report* an-nual college issue from 2000 contains a series of useful questions cate-gorized as "questions to ask of students" and "questions to ask of administrators." In addition to the usual ones, such as, "Where do students study?" and essential ones on campus safety, my personal favorites to be directed at administrators are, "What was your average cost increase in tuition over the past five years?" and "What are the incidental costs on campus?"[12]

A PLANNING CHECKLIST

The National Association for College Admission Counseling (NACAC) is an association of secondary school and college and university admission counselors who work with students making the transition from high school to postsecondary education. NACAC's user-friendly Web site (www.nacac.com) contains several features helpful to students planning college visits. Parents may also find the site useful in planning a college visit with a son or daughter. The following checklist was created by NACAC and is available from the organization's Web site:

Formal
- Take a campus tour
- Have an interview with an admissions officer
- Participate in a group information session at the admissions office
- Sit in on a class (or two!)
- Talk to a professor (or two) in your [possible] major(s)
- Talk to a coach in your chosen sport
- Talk to a student or counselor in the career center
- Spend the night in the dorm with a current student

Informal
- Read the student newspaper—including the ads
- Try to find other student publications—department newsletters, "alternative" newspapers, literary reviews
- Eat in the cafeteria
- Ask a student why he/she chose this college
- Wander around the campus by yourself

- Search for your favorite book in the library
- Read the bulletin boards in the student union
- Ask a student what he/she hates about the college
- Browse in the college bookstore
- Read the bulletin boards in the academic department you are interested in
- Eavesdrop on students to hear what they are talking—or complaining—about
- Ask a student what he/she loves about the college
- Surf the Web in the student computer center
- Walk or drive around the community surrounding the campus
- Ask a student what he/she does on weekends
- Listen to the college's radio station
- Try to see a dorm that you did not see on the [official] tour
- See if you can imagine yourself at this college[13]

Letting Your Child Take the Lead

When visiting colleges and, for that matter, throughout most of the admissions process, it is essential that parents let their child take the lead. Parents should try to keep a low profile during college tours. While admissions officers welcome questions from parents, the parents on the tour should not dominate the conversation. Parents need to remember that this is a time for their child to make his or her own observations about the school.

College tour guides, the undergraduate students who escort families around campus during the college visit, see it all. Several tour guides I interviewed at colleges in the Boston area during the 2000–2001 school year noted that the students tend to ask few if any questions, while the parents come prepared, sometimes with lists of questions.[14] It is as if the parents and the students have polar agendas when visiting the colleges. The parents' focus tends to be on the practical, the students' on the emotional. Parents want to know how much things cost, how safe are the dorms and the neighborhood around the campus, and how new is the technology in the library. Students look at the gym, the Greek houses or campus clubs, the sports program, the local restaurants and bars, and the students. All the tour guides I spoke with only wish they could speak quietly, and alone, to the prospective students.

VIDEOCONFERENCING AND THE INTERNET

In the past, high school students who wanted information on a college had to read the brochure from the guidance counselor's office, turn to Peterson's or one of the other college guidebooks, or visit the campus. Next, students and parents were able to log onto the college's Web site. Now, an increasing number of colleges are experimenting with videoconferencing to answer applicants' (and parents') questions about their school.[15] Videoconferencing technology permits college applicants and admissions officers to meet face-to-face in cyberspace.

Already, it seems, many Americans are comfortable with the Internet as an unparalleled research tool. In helping her son, a junior at the Horace Mann School in Riverdale, New York, search for schools, Belle Frank has found that the college Web sites that offer on-line insider guides (student-written frequently asked questions features) are typically more informative than the college Web sites that do not offer such features.[16] Many of the prospective college parents and students with whom I spoke tended to be put off by hard-to-navigate Web sites. Ms. Frank and her son noted the need to remind themselves when researching schools that a bad or good Web site does not necessarily correspond with a bad or good school. The Franks and the other parents and students with whom I spoke were also keen to the fact that the Web site is the college putting its best foot forward and presenting itself through its own rose-colored glasses. Before they settle on a school, the Franks plan to visit the campus, preferably when classes are in session, as well as continue their research on-line with help from Horace Mann's college counselor, speak with current and former students, and peruse the several college guidebooks they have already purchased or checked out of the local library.

In those cases in which cost or infirmity may prevent a family from visiting a college in person, the Web may also serve as an effective alternative to being there. The relative infancy of Internet technology makes it hard to predict just how widespread this medium will become and whether it will ever replace live visits to colleges by prospective students. However, given the explosive growth and appeal of the Internet as a means of conducting background research on virtually everything, we may expect to see more families making their first visit to schools on-line.

SPECIAL SERVICES

In recent years, the Princeton Review, a well-established college test preparation company, and Achieva.com, a late-1990s start-up, as well as several other lesser-known companies, have created intensive, parent-friendly programs to assist teens in researching, applying to, and preparing for college. The Achieva Nine-Step Advantage Program, for example, is advertised as a program that will give you and your child the following:

- step-by-step guidance through every phase of the college admissions process
- admissions information on every four-year college or university

Whether the student seeks to attend a highly selective university or a local or state college, both the Princeton Review and Achieva programs claim to guide students through the process. According to Achieva, its program provides information to help applicants do the following:

- tap into their strengths and interests to realize their full potential

- identify what college admissions officers are looking for
- complete applications and the proper supplemental materials including recommendations, essays, and financial aid forms
- adhere to college admission deadlines

A word of caution. Whether companies like Achieva are selling snake oil to the public or providing parents and their college-bound son or daughter with an important and valuable service remains to be seen by consumers. Some of these businesses are simply too new for a fair assessment of their products and services. Caveat emptor, or let the buyer beware, would be advisable for parents, especially with the less-established programs. As with any other purchase, consumers of college preparation services should first consult a reliable consumer products and services rating guide such as *Consumer Reports* or other business reference resources. Without irony, I quote a popular New York advertising slogan in which the company owner concludes, "An educated consumer is our best customer." Find out as much as you can about the different college preparation courses so you can make an informed decision between programs or about whether such courses will truly suit your son's or daughter's needs.

A PULSE AND A CHECKBOOK

With the exception of the country's most selective institutions, most colleges and universities are praying that your child wants to spend the next four to five years on their campuses. As is the case in so many other businesses, to stay alive in higher education a school needs a fresh pool of new customers every year: living, breathing clients with hearts that beat and checkbooks that can pay tuition bills. Increasingly, credit cards are also accepted. Just because a school wants your child, however, does not mean that it should get him or her. Our role as parents is to help our children select colleges that are right for them.

Parents, of course, should be relieved to know that most schools want their child. In fact, most schools inundate accepted students with brochures, e-mails, and other promotional material designed to convince the student, and the student's parents, that he or she would be a fool to attend college anywhere else.

According to a May 3, 2000, article in the *New York Times,* "The thirty days from April 1, when such offers are generally proffered, to May 1, when such decisions are due, is a time unlike any other in the college admissions season, at least for a select group of several thousand students." During this brief window, accepted students "become the decision makers, screening potential candidates against a yardstick of their own idiosyncrasies, while [college admissions] officers are reduced to supplicants, promoting their schools as they brace for rejections from many of those they wanted most." Rafael Figueroa, an associate dean of admissions at Wesleyan University in Connecticut, told the *Times,* "It is a courting period," during which admissions officers at some select private colleges feel that "they are pursuing many of the same fifteen hundred teenagers." The article goes on to quote a highly sought-after college-bound student who says, "I feel like a Michael Jordan trading card from his rookie season. . . . The schools are putting in a lot of effort to get me while I'm in mint condition."[17]

As if applying to college were not anxiety-producing enough, for students accepted to more than one elite college, fear of choosing the wrong school weighs heavily as well. According to Ms. Frank, the Horace Mann parent, for many competitive students the decision becomes all-consuming and the stress can carry over to the rest of the family.[18] With her son still a year and a half away from college, Ms. Frank is trying to remain supportive but as removed as she can be from her son's final decision making about which schools to go for.

To many families, including the Franks, who live in an affluent community and send their children to private school, parents today are generally more involved than they were in the past in their children's college screening process.

ADMISSIONS: YOU'RE NOT DONE YET

As obsequiousness has become the norm, schools that overlook candidates after they have been accepted tend to lose them. Karen Zweig, mother of a junior at Tufts University in Medford, Massachusetts, describes how her son had been hoping to attend a well-regarded private university in Atlanta until he took a closer look at his pool of acceptances.[19] While Tufts wooed him, the Atlanta school from which he had been most pleased to receive an acceptance letter now seemed to view him as just another student. While the environmentalist in me mourns the waste of paper and ink, schools *should* be fawning over your college-bound child. He or she *is* special, and the attention is most deserved.

Money, discussed in detail in chapter 2, is another way a college can show it cares about your son or daughter. Smart schools may seek to match or best a financial aid grant that has been offered by another admissions office to woo your child to attend their college, though I have yet to find an admissions officer willing to be quoted in print as having made such an offer. Just because a school does not offer to up their financial aid package doesn't mean you can't ask them to. Once your child has that admissions letter, he or she is in the driver's seat and anything that saves you both on tuition is hard-earned money saved.

ATHLETIC RECRUITING

Many are called; few are chosen. This can surely be said of college athletes. A June 21, 2000, article in the *Boston Globe* describes a college recruit's nine hundred letters received from interested schools over the first three years of high school. "Unless it's handwritten, I put it in this stack. You can sort of tell who's sincere and who's not," explains the much sought-after high school athlete pointing to a pile of unopened letters.[20] One word to parents and students about athletic recruiting: unless your son or daughter is the next Drew Bledsoe, Mia Hamm, or Isiah Thomas, in seeking a college, take the recruiters' aggressive pitches with a healthy dose of skepticism. As good an athlete as your child may be, schools and their scouts have many high school juniors and seniors in their sights. Once they have found and landed the best prospects, colleges tend to drop the others rather quickly. For those not chosen by their preferred school, the emotional letdown can be profound. Parents can help their son or daughter avoid the disappointment by tempering their enthusiasm from all the initial attention. A parent whose son or daughter is being pursued because of his or her athletic achievements needs to recognize that college athletics is big business.

College athletics can indeed greatly influence and perhaps even define a school. As a result, the pressures on student athletes at schools with aggressive, highly regarded athletic programs can be tremendous. But, at such schools, the pressures may also weigh heavily on nonathletes. For example, parents and students alike may want to consider visiting a big football or basketball school on a game weekend so they can, of course, attend a game, but also so they can see some of the downside of attending a place where athletics defines the culture. Although I am likely to catch flack from my own alma mater, the University of Michigan, on this one, parents and students should consider just how disruptive a game weekend can be to the campus and the community. With the pregame parties in full steam the night before a game, you may find yourself asking, doesn't anyone in this town sleep at night? And where did all those beer cans and bottles on the curb come from if three-quarters of the undergraduates are underage? Is this the sort of place your son or daughter is looking for? Or would a school less obsessed with football or basketball be a better place for your child to get an education?

Of even greater concern are the types of problems that have occurred at several universities that pride themselves on their outstanding athletic programs. According to a May 21, 2000, article in the *New York Times,*

In recent years, officials at the University of Minnesota and the University of Tennessee have struggled with allegations of academic fraud by athletes, while the University of Nebraska dealt with accusations that star football players physically abused women. The University of Vermont canceled part of the hockey season [during the 1999–2000 school year] because of hazing, and Providence College expelled three basketball players . . . over an assault.[21]

Parents and students going through the application process will also want to know how a particular school with a disgraceful incident has gone about addressing its problems. Some would say, for example, that Providence College and the University of Vermont took far more vigorous and appropriate approaches to their problems than did Indiana, which only fired Bobby Knight, its notoriously rogue coach, after his nth warning from the school. Before Indiana finally fired Knight its tolerance of his abhorrent behavior seemed to send the message that athletics are more important than academics at the Big Ten school. Meanwhile, Reverend Philip A. Smith, the president of Providence College, a small Roman Catholic school in Rhode Island, had expelled three players and is quoted in the *New York Times* as saying, "An assault on a student goes to the very heart of who we are. This is not a basketball issue for me."[22] Similarly, with support from the governor and the state attorney general, the University of Vermont (UVM) canceled the remainder of the college hockey season in January 2000 following the hazing incident (the college hockey season would have ended in March). Vermont's governor expressed outrage at the hazing incident and got involved as an ex officio member of the university's Board of Trustees when the university did not initially move to act against the team and the players involved. UVM officials then asked the state attorney general to investigate the charges. Under oath, several members of the hockey team admitted they had not told the truth earlier and provided details. UVM's president Judith Ramaley then canceled the remainder of the season.

WE WORK HARD AND PLAY HARD. . . .

Watch out. Any school that boasts this mentality does not deserve the attention of serious students and conscientious candidates, including your child. "Playing hard" does not refer to the school's athletic program. As the evening news has demonstrated these past few years, a school that portrays itself as hard working and hard drinking is a catastrophe waiting to happen.

Take, for example, the case of Washington State University (WSU), which has suffered several embarrassing incidents in recent years, including a student riot in 1998 and ongoing problems at some of its fraternities. In an April 16, 2000, article on Spokane.net, University of Washington police captain and WSU alumnus Randy Stegmeier noted, "As an institution, WSU has suffered a major black eye."[23] Regent Ken Alhadeff and other WSU officials also express their concerns that a pervasive party school image will hurt recruitment, attract students who are not serious about education, and devalue the degrees of those who are. WSU faces the prospect of being a good school with a bad image. At a school like WSU, where female students have posed for *Playboy* with the school pennant as a backdrop, a good deal of press attention has focused on out-of-control fraternities, and the effects of the riot linger in the media. The gravity of WSU's image problem is best expressed by enlightened parents who say, "I don't know if I want to send my kids to a school known as party central."

Whether you like it or not, college life has changed considerably over the last two decades. First came Ronald and Nancy Reagan and the appallingly patronizing and simplistic "Just Say No" assault on drug use among children. Next came the narrow focus on character education in the elementary and secondary schools. Now, many college administrators are asking what should be a college's role, if any, in teaching character to its students. In my experience, the answer to this question involves well-executed enforcement strategies targeted at unacceptable and aberrant student behaviors such as dangerous drinking, date rape, and bias crimes against gay or minority students on the campus. For example, a growing number of colleges (including Washington and Lee University in Virginia and Colby College in Maine) are exploring ways to terminate the leases of campus housing for fraternities and sororities that have become the source of trouble and embarrassment because of out-of-control parties. Commonly, the colleges themselves own the houses and lease them to the fraternities. All too often, the sort of activities in which members engage is grounds for a termination of the lease. While the Greeks will not go without a public relations battle and a legal challenge, situations of this sort represent just the kind of case that colleges will want to take on. These are the win-win cases that get rid of the offending fraternity and send a message to the campus and community at large that this sort of behavior will not be tolerated.

Law professor Peter Lake of Stetson University College of Law in Florida advises parents of college-bound students to carefully consider the realities of heavy student drinking at prospective colleges:

> Strict policies aimed at high-risk or underage drinking sometime coexist with high rates of high-risk alcohol use—so-called "binge drinking." Thus, a school with tough policies is not necessarily one with a safer culture; in fact, my work has shown that patterns of high-risk alcohol use mutate very quickly around disciplinary rules aimed at those patterns. For instance, it is not uncommon for students to pack up and move their high-risk drinking off campus to avoid tougher on-campus rules, or to leave highly regulated fraternities in favor of living arrangements—usually off campus—that are more conducive to out-of-control partying. Therefore, parents and students must be proactive and carefully consider the drinking culture at colleges being considered.[24]

CHARACTER DEVELOPMENT

On the opposite end of the spectrum from the party schools are the growing number of colleges that are setting new standards for character education and public service. In a speech as a guest lecturer at Yale University in 1999, University of Pennsylvania President Judith Rodin said the following:

It is not enough to provide a great education. . . . It is not enough for us to produce brilliant, imaginative doctors, lawyers, scholars, and scientists who will press the envelopes of their disciplines or professions, if we do not also engage them in the larger issues of our day, in the ferment of our times and our society.[25]

Tufts University, outside of Boston, started the University College of Citizenship and Public Service in 1999 with a $10 million start-up grant from Pierre Omidyar, a Tufts graduate and the founder of eBay, the on-line auction site. The grant will pay for scholarships, faculty development, and a venture fund for community projects over the next five years. The goal of the Tufts program is to transform public service from a few hours of tutoring poor children or working in a homeless shelter to a lifelong commitment to civic engagement—regardless of the student's chosen profession after graduation. Following is the *New York Times* description of the Tufts program:

the most comprehensive example [to date] of the efforts being made by hundreds of universities across the nation to re-emphasize public service as a core tenet of the curriculum. Though more college students than ever do volunteer work while on campus, according to the Vanishing Voter Project at Harvard University, voter participation among 18- to 24-year-olds is at an all-time low. The new movement tries to combat the commodification of higher education, to reassert its goal as creating responsible citizens rather than training students for jobs.[26]

Terry W. Hartle, senior vice president of the American Council on Education, which represents some 3,500 institutions, is cited in the *Times* article as saying, "Historically, this has been a central purpose of higher education. But in the current sociopolitical environment, it's a very difficult undertaking." [27]

In response to the need for renewed emphasis on public service across the country, an organization known as Campus Compact was established in 1985. According to this national association comprising 670 colleges and universities devoted to community service, 374,000 students nationally performed 32 million hours of volunteer work in 1999.[28]

In selecting a college, parents and students might also want to consider some of the hundreds of universities that are trying to set an example of good citizenship themselves by forming partnerships with their local towns and cities focusing on such issues as affordable housing, literacy, and environmental cleanup projects.

In recent years, a number of college and university presidents, including outgoing Tufts University President John DiBiaggio, have restated their schools' educational missions to include character development and service learning. Dr. DiBiaggio's rewrite of Tufts's vision statement emphasizes the goals of fostering an attitude of "giving back" and "a desire to make the world a better place."[29]

With character education a leading subject of discussion among university leaders and other experts in the field of higher education, a guide to colleges that encourage character development was overdue. *Colleges That Encourage Character Development: A Resource for Parents, Students, and Educators,* or *The Templeton Guide,* considers 405 colleges in several categories including

- student leadership programs
- spiritual growth programs
- civic education programs
- character and sexuality programs[30]

While scholarly in appearance and handsomely laid out and bound, *The Templeton Guide* is somewhat similar to the *Who's Who in America* collections that rely on self-promotion and the limited expertise of a small group of leading authorities from the field. Additionally, the guide's conservative, religious orientation will not appeal to all readers. Others, though, may find the book helpful especially when used in conjunction with a guide that includes information on accreditation, degrees offered, and college costs.

DISTANCE LEARNING

Recent advancements in education technology have led to a number of new methods of delivering education to students beyond the gates of the college campus. At the forefront of the distance learning movement is the University of California, which is designing its newest branch to go where the students are because students cannot always afford to come to its campuses.[31] The university's new campus at Merced is set to open in 2004, and in addition to offering classes on campus, the new university will be the first of several distributed-learning centers intended to bring top-quality education to residents of central California. Eventually, centers will be located in other central California cities as well.

According to the University of California, distributed-learning centers rely on technology to make available the same quality courses that are available on the main campus, so students will be able to take some of their courses while living at home and will only have to attend classes on campus for a portion of the time it takes to earn a degree at Merced, which could ultimately save money on things like room and board. The institution is being planned as a full-scale research university with a projected enrollment of about six thousand on-campus and off-campus students by 2010.[32]

In California and other states where distance learning is all the rage, one big question has been whether there will be sufficient demand for the new teaching technology, which can be quite costly to implement (California's new university will cost about $250 million just to build).[33] However, the impact of distance learning on the college experience has yet to be determined. Many administrators, perhaps reflecting their financial vulnerability, remain highly critical of the pedagogy. In an interview with me in January 2001, Matthew S. Santirocco, dean of the College of Arts and Sciences at New York University explained, "Distance learning and for-profit universities are delivering one product. Our kind of university is delivering something different, a model of community with mentoring and classroom interaction."[34]

So what does distance learning mean for parents of college-bound students? For those students who choose to remain at home and learn from a distance, many of the issues facing parents of students leaving home to attend school vanish. Indeed, many parents may welcome the new educational model for the flexibility and cost savings it may offer.

TRANSFER STUDENTS

No matter how hard they try, not all college-bound students make the right college choice the first time. A number of factors account for this, not the least of which is parents projecting their own goals and preferences onto their children.

Selecting a college is a head and a heart thing. It's not just a rational choice, but also an emotional one. Before your child starts school, he or she won't know if the chosen college is going to be the right one. Also, no one can know the road not taken. A transfer may be the best course of action if the student finds that the college picked has let the student down or if the student has changed majors.

In addition, many who transfer schools are making the transition from two- to four-year schools. According to an on-line article in *U.S. News and World Report,* some 46 percent of the nearly 2.7 million first-time freshmen enroll in two-year colleges. About a quarter of those students later transfer to four-year colleges.[35]

Both students and parents need to be aware that transfer acceptance rates vary greatly from college to college. Before applying, students should find out the acceptance rate for the sought-after school.

Being older and wiser than our children, parents may also want to gently explore with a child interested in transferring whether he or she really is going to be happier and better off at the new school. By talking with your child about his or her decision to switch schools, you may be able to learn more about the motivation behind the planned change. Parents, for instance, may be able to help a first-year student get past homesickness or other temporary hurdles and thereby help the student realize that transferring schools may not be the solution to the problem. Where depression or a disturbing experience at college is behind the student's desire to transfer, parents may also be able to get at such issues through talks with the student about his or her motivation.[36] Those students in need of professional help can then receive the attention they deserve.

Adjusting to a new environment, making new friends, and learning about the culture of the new school are all significant challenges that transfer students tend to gloss over when going through the application process. Among those who do decide to transfer, some students will find that attending the new school's freshman orientation helps with some of the logistical issues. Others find that starting out with summer school is a good way to become acclimated to the new campus before other students return to school. For parents, a child's transferring may mean new, unanticipated college costs, particularly if a student's college credits don't transfer to the new school.

Being aware of these various transfer issues may help with the adjustment process.

OH, THE PLACES YOU'LL GO!

Like the character in the classic *Oh, the Places You'll Go* by Dr. Seuss:

> Congratulations!
> Today is your day.
> You're off to Great Places!
> You're off and away![37]

In undertaking the college selection process together, you and your son or daughter are off on an exciting adventure sure to be filled with ups and downs and many in-between emotions. As you move through this book and through the entire college selection process, be sure to laugh and smile at all the crazy things you will undoubtedly see, hear, and, think. And when you are done, rest assured that this book will be near, like Dr. Seuss, with "advice [though not in rhyme] for proceeding in [college parent] life; weathering fear, loneliness, and confusion, and being in charge of your actions."[38]

TWO

Paying for College and Getting What You Pay For

■ ■ ■

All those who like to pay bills for thousands of dollars please stop reading now. For all of the rest of the parents in the real world, let's move on to a discussion of how you are going to pay or help pay for your son's or daughter's college education. And in case you were wondering, college tuition is *not* tax deductible.

Although hardly a new concern, in recent years, the high cost of American higher education has driven a growing number of parents and students to view a college education much as they would other commodities they might wish to purchase. A consumer's movement has emerged in the higher education area, challenging colleges to examine their educational missions and philosophies, as well as their balance sheets. In most cases, we, as parents, are making a major financial "investment" when sending a child off to college. Diane Schulman, a consumer affairs producer at WBZ-TV in Boston and the mother of a college senior, puts it this way, "Many people don't spend that much on a house."[1]

PLANNING TO PAY FOR COLLEGE

According to the National Center for Education Statistics, in 1998, the mean cost for tuition and fees at a four-year public college or university was $3,073. For a private university, the cost was $11,239.

Figuring in room and board, the costs rise to $7,209 for public universities and $16,084 for private institutions.[2] Indeed, in New England, many families are now paying upwards of $40,000 a year to send each of their children to college. Given these numbers, paying for college, for all but the richest Americans, presents a significant challenge.

No one said that paying for college would be fun, nor would reading about it. If you just can't bear to read this section, please skim it and remember that every September many local and national newspapers run big spreads on college money matters. Additionally, you may want to research the issue on the Web, which offers a wealth of information about financing a college education. One excellent Web site, www.SavingForCollege.com, offers up-to-date information about state tuition plans under federal Internal Revenue Code, section 529. Joe Hurley, founder of the Web site, has also authored a useful book called *The Best Way to Save for College.*

PREPAID TUITION PLANS AND SAVINGS PLAN TRUSTS

There are two forms of college savings programs offered in many states: prepaid tuition plans and savings plan trusts. According to Miles A. Rubin, a vice president of investments at Paine Webber in New York City, most *prepaid tuition plans* allow participants to begin paying college tuition costs when the future student is still an infant.[3]

Although inflation rates are running nationally at a 2 to 3 percent rate, private college tuitions are rising at closer to 6 to 7 percent a year. A child born in 2000 can levy a tuition bill on his or her parents of over $100,000 per year by the time he or she goes off to school. Prepaid tuition plans lock their participants into the tuition price being charged at the state's public colleges in the year when a student is enrolled in the plan. Typically, the plans guarantee to pay for tuition at in-state public colleges and universities regardless of how much the cost has risen since the beneficiary enrolled. According to Rubin, payments to these prepaid plans can be made monthly or can be paid by the participant in a lump sum.[4]

Additionally, sometimes the funds may be used to pay tuition at an accredited private or out-of-state college. Under prepaid tuition plans offered by certain states, if the participant goes to a private or out-of-state college, the participant is responsible for paying the difference between the current price of tuition at the private or out-of-state school and the original prepaid tuition price.

The federal tax on a prepaid tuition plan, as well as the income generated through plan investments, is deferrable until the funds are used to pay for college. At that point the money is taxed at the student's then-current tax rate, which is extremely beneficial because the student's tax rate is typically the lowest tax rate possible.

Savings plan trusts, explains Rubin, are investment accounts that parents can use to save for their children's education.[5] Trust plan participants can make deposits of as little as $25. The programs usually guarantee a minimum rate of return, and the funds may be used at any accredited U.S. college or university. Unlike prepaid tuition plans, savings plan trusts do not guarantee tuition regardless of a rise in tuition prices. However, these savings plans may pay higher returns on investments than prepaid tuition plans. Like prepaid plans, funds in these trusts are federally tax deferrable until the student enters college and are then taxed at the student's current tax rate. Both types of plans also receive state tax benefits. These benefits will vary from state to state.

State residency requirements are common among savings plan trusts. Such requirements usually dictate that either the participant or the student must be a state resident when the student is first enrolled in the savings plan trust.

FINANCIAL AID — THE ABCS OF EFCS

With college costs prohibitively high for many families, financial aid is often the help that makes it possible for the student to attend school. Financial aid is defined loosely as the dollars and cents of support colleges make available to students who have received an offer of acceptance. Jeffrey M. Sherman, a private investment manager at Tucker Anthony in Wellesley, Massachusetts, advises families to start their financial planning as early as possible—particularly those who intend to apply for financial aid. As part of the financial aid application process, each applicant is provided with an Expected Family Contribution (EFC) for their son's or daughter's college.[6] This is the actual amount the family will need to pay for the child's education. March 1 is the financial aid deadline at many schools. Once the forms are calculated, families are mailed back a student aid report, which includes the EFC. Sherman notes that most families do not have a clue what EFC means until the student applies for financial aid.

Another way a family can learn its EFC is by completing either the Free Application for Federal Student Aid (FAFSA) or the College Board's CSS/Profile.[7] The College Board's profile is a detailed application used by 350 mostly private colleges and universities to disburse their own financial aid. While some families have become skilled at making themselves look as needy as possible to secure the most financial aid, challenging the way the EFC is calculated is not going to be successful.

Although the FAFSA and CSS/Profile differ from one another in a number of ways, both expect contributions from the parents' income and assets as well as from the students themselves. Under the federal formula, the parents' contribution is calculated at roughly 6 percent of their cash, savings (other than retirement accounts), and real estate equity (other than a primary residence). The rate for students for any assets is a considerably higher rate of 35 percent. According to the College Board, how much a family ends up contributing out of pocket is generally far more dependent on income than assets.

QUALIFIED STATE TUITION PLANS

In a February 2001 interview, Rand Hutcheson, a lawyer in the Estate Planning Group at Rackemann, Sawyer, and Brewster, a Boston law firm, noted that, in general, you can pay a child's or grandchild's tuition free of any gift tax if you pay it directly to the educational institution involved. This type of financial planning, called prepaid state tuition plans, allows parents or others to pay for a child's future education at today's tuition prices. Typically, these plans allow for tax-deferred growth of far larger sums than do educational IRAs. State tuition plans place no restrictions on how much a person can contribute, allowing for substantial sums to be set aside in a single year.

A former college professor, Hutcheson succinctly explains the advantages and disadvantages of qualified state tuition plans under section 529 of the Internal Revenue Code (IRC) as follows.

Advantages

- *Annual exclusions:* you can use up to five years' worth of annual gift tax exclusions in one year. In other words, you can put $50,000 per child into a qualified state tuition plan ($100,000 for married couples who decide to split gifts) tax-free, as long as you do not make any other taxable gifts to the child for five years.
- *Tax deferral:* growth in the plan is not taxed until the funds are taken out, at which point the funds are taxed as ordinary income at the child's income tax rate.[8]

As of January 2001, qualified section 529 plans were available in forty-eight states, with most offering two types of investment programs: a prepaid tuition plan that lets you set aside money for your child's college education at today's rates (as explained earlier in this chapter) and second, a plan that invests your money in a managed portfolio of stocks, bonds, and money market funds.[9]

Disadvantages

- The "tax advantage" might not be so advantageous; if the same funds were invested in growth equities, the only thing that would be taxed as ordinary income would be the

dividends (which would be taxed at the parents' rates).
Tax on capital appreciation would be deferred until the equities are sold, at which time they would be taxed at capital
gains rates (which probably would not be too different from
the ordinary income rates for the child under the qualified
plan).

- Investors cannot choose investments, which are selected by
the plan.
- Funds must be used for "qualified higher education expenses," which include "tuition, fees, books, supplies, and
equipment required for the enrollment or attendance of a
designated beneficiary at an eligible educational institution"
(section 529[e][3][A]). Generally, the definition of an "eligible
educational institution" excludes institutions outside the
United States.[10]

UNIFORM TRANSFERS TO MINORS ACT (UTMA) ACCOUNTS

Hutcheson notes that for those who can afford to make a relatively
large gift to a minor to pay for college, the UTMA account permits
the donor and custodian to give up to $10,000 per year ($20,000 for a
married couple that chooses to split gifts) to each child as a tax-free
gift. The child who receives the gift is granted full access to the
funds at age twenty-one (or as early as age eighteen in some states).
Another important fact about this type of account is that the custodian chooses the investments, but if the custodian should die before
the child reaches age twenty-one, the accounts will be included in
the custodian's taxable estate. If the child is under age fourteen, all
income in the account over a certain amount ($1,500) is taxed at
the parents' tax rate (see Internal Revenue Code, section 1[g] for
details).[11]

U.S. SAVINGS BONDS

Remember these? Income from U.S. savings bonds, notes Hutcheson, is tax-free if it is used for qualified higher education expenses.[12] This option will only appeal to the most conservative investors.

EDUCATIONAL IRAS

Educational IRAs have an annual donation cap of $500. Given the high cost of college this option is of limited value.

IRREVOCABLE EDUCATIONAL TRUSTS

These are general, legally binding trust instruments that cannot be changed and that can receive gifts to remove assets from the donor's estate. The trusts can be limited to educational purposes or can be more broadly written.

According to Rand Hutcheson, there are three important advantages to irrevocable educational trusts:

- This type of trust can be funded with annual exclusion gifts of $10,000 (or $20,000 a year for a married couple) per beneficiary, free of any gift tax.
- Upon your death, the trust's assets would not be included in your estate nor would there be any gift, estate, or generation-skipping transfer taxes on such a trust if properly planned.
- The trust could pay any educational expenses (tuition, room, board, books, etc.) at any educational institution in the world, *as well as other expenses of the beneficiary* (i.e., expenses need not be limited solely to educational expenses).

Irrevocable educational trusts have two principal disadvantages:

- the expense of drafting and administration
- there are no particular income tax advantages, other than that income passed through to a beneficiary is taxed at the beneficiary's tax rate (subject to the same restrictions that apply to UTMA accounts)[13]

SCHOLARSHIPS

There are Scholarships and then there are scholarships. In the former category are the Rhodes, Rotary, and, perhaps soon, Bill and Melinda Gates scholarships. The focus here is on the little "s" scholarship programs that can help a student make ends meet and are available to a much larger pool of eligible applicants. The fact is, as costly as it is to attend college, many college-bound students are leaving money on the table that they could be using to pay down their all-too-soon coming due student loans.

Deborah Hahn, Ph.D., assistant dean for undergraduate academic affairs at Brandeis University in Waltham, Massachusetts, notes that millions of dollars in scholarship money are never distributed because many students do not know how to go after them and receive scant grooming and advice from their schools on how to apply.[14] According to Hahn, many colleges, including her own, have created a staff position in the dean's office aimed at assisting eligible students to identify and apply for scholarships. While prestigious awards like the Rhodes and Rotary scholarships usually require nomination and are often limited to students planning to pursue graduate degrees in designated fields, many other scholarship programs are less selective. Given a student with the right stuff (e.g., excellent grades and an exceptional commitment to community service), success in obtaining a scholarship is often a matter of research, packaging, and volume—the more scholarships applied for, the greater the likelihood of obtaining an award.

Parents and students interested in academic and other scholarships may find it useful to review college catalogs with an eye to the schools' emphasis on awards. Does the catalog note how many scholarship winners attended the college in the prior year? Does the catalog include a description of how the college identifies students who may be promising candidates for scholarships? A number of schools place considerable emphasis on the support and expertise they can offer to students interested in pursuing scholarship monies and programs.

Additionally, local scholarships are good places for students to start. Many foundations target their awards to students from a particular geographic area, ethnic group, or field of study. These tend to be relatively modest, such as one-time grants of $2,500 limited to students with a demonstrated financial need. Of course, with college costs exceeding $40,000 a year at many schools, demonstrating financial need is becoming easier and easier for many candidates.

Though not foolproof, the Web is a great source of information on scholarships. *U.S. News and World Report* has a "find a scholarship" function on its college Web site (www.usnews.com/usnews/edu/dollars/scholar/search.htm). The Web site lets you conduct quick searches for scholarships based on categories such as ethnicity, athletics, art, corporations, organizations, and the military. The site also permits the user to search for scholarships by keyword or phrase such as the award name, school name, organization, or corporation issuing the award. For example, you may search for the phrase "Duke" if you are interested in scholarships for students of Duke University, or you may search for "Levi Strauss" if you are interested in scholarships offered to children of Levi Strauss employees. When searching, use full names. Abbreviations such as "MIT" will not work.

STUDENT EMPLOYMENT—WILL WORK FOR MONEY

The Basics

A basic premise governing need-based financial aid programs is that families have the primary responsibility to pay for college costs. Part of this expectation is that students, to the extent that they are able, should help pay for their college expenses. Student employment, both during the academic year and over the summers, can make an important contribution to a student's financial resources.

The chart below, based on one prepared by the financial aid office at the University of Michigan, shows how working a modest number of hours can provide income during the thirty weeks of the academic year. The rate of pay is based on the current average hourly rate at the University of Michigan for temporary jobs.

Hours per Week at $6/hour (Academic Year)

8 hours	$1,440
12 hours	$2,160
15 hours	$2,700[15]

Since most college-bound students' dot-com stock options have yet to vest, or worse yet, have already tanked, many students will find it necessary to work while attending college. Parents concerned that work will interfere with a child's studies should remember the adage "if you want something done right, give it to a busy person." According to William DeJong, Ph.D., director of the U.S. Department of Education's Higher Education Center for Alcohol and Other Drug Prevention, most students have a great deal of free time on their hands.[16] Students who work during college tend to develop a stronger appreciation of the value of their education than those for whom education is fully paid. Working students generally tend to work *and* study hard, and master the art of juggling responsibilities better than students whose parents shelter their children from financial responsibility. Given the choice, I always hire a busy person over someone with few adult responsibilities.

The University of Michigan Web site (www.umich.edu) deals with the issue of students working during the academic year. Comparing students who do not work to students who work a modest number of hours per week—no more than fifteen—the students who have paying jobs will, on average,

- have higher grade point averages
- graduate at a faster rate

- be less likely to drop out
- have important job skills to include on their resumes

Why is this so? Some possible explanations are as follows:

- Working students become better organized and manage their time better.
- Employment exposes students to more mentor-type relationships and increases interactions with "real world" people.
- Employment is critical to meeting college costs.[17]

Many colleges go to great lengths to help students identify on- and off-campus jobs. The University of Michigan, for instance, has prepared a helpful Web site detailing work available to students, (www.finaid.umich.edu/employ.htm). Similar information is available for most schools through the college Web site or through the campus student employment office.

Work-Study Jobs

Work-study offers students part-time work with employers who qualify for funding under federal or state guidelines when participating in a school's work-study program. These work-study jobs are usually listed with the financial aid office and are awarded to those students with the greatest financial need. Work-study students are some of the most highly sought-after employees, on- and off-campus, because federal or state funding covers 75 percent of the wage rate, while the employer (usually university departments or an off-campus nonprofit organization) pays only 25 percent. Students interested in community service positions may find a number of jobs available through the work-study program (listed as "Community Service" within the work-study Web postings).

Temporary or Part-Time Jobs On- or Off-Campus

Although not everyone parlays their part-time college job into a lucrative career, working during college can help young persons begin to identify areas that interest them or, in rare cases, get started on the next Netscape. Gordon M. Henry, a vice president for business development with i-Open, a start-up dot-com in Philadelphia, encourages college students to be aware of emerging business opportunities while in school and to look for colleges that encourage students to work and seem to foster entrepreneurship.[18] He notes the inspirational examples of Microsoft and Dell, two highly successful computer companies that were both conceived in college dorm rooms. Striking it rich as an entrepreneur while still in college will also make Mom and Dad happy, so be sure to get your child thinking about the next Microsoft while he or she is still at home.

By now you may have noticed that I am partial to the University of Michigan's student employment Web site. Go Blue! Yes, I *am* a graduate and fan. Currently, the university and the city of Ann Arbor where the school is located are enjoying a robust employment market. Students willing to work can find jobs! At Michigan and many other schools, the university library system and the housing information office are always in search of good employees—and these are just two of the many departments employing students. At many colleges, students can visit a student employment Web site to view local and campus job listings.

CREDIT CARDS

Another way that students try to make ends meet in college is by obtaining and using a credit card. Both students and parents need to beware of the credit card companies that litter college and university campuses with their seductive offers. Sure, credit cards are convenient, but, in my opinion, no son or daughter should get one before he or she is ready to pay the bills. According to college freshmen I interviewed in Boston, Ithaca, and Philadelphia, the card companies keep bothering students with promotional offers until they just couldn't say no. Despite their lack of credit history and limited incomes, college students are viewed as gold mines by the credit card companies.

Eager to establish a credit history and become financially independent from their parents, some college students are easy prey to credit card company marketers who bombard the students with advertising. Cards are tied in with clothing companies, airlines (free tickets), and electronic equipment. Of course, easy credit is not a threat to college students alone. Consumer protection advocates have long chastised the financial services industry for marketing their products to individuals who may not be prepared to use them responsibly. But to some, the pitch to college students is particularly galling. According to Robert D. Manning, a visiting professor of sociology at Georgetown University, it is harder to get credit after graduation than it is if you have never had a job and you are a full-time student. Dr. Manning warns that the credit card industry has sought to create the impression that credit cards are plastic money rather than debt.[19] Student Monitor, a New Jersey–based marketing research firm, notes that more than half of students at four-year colleges have at least one credit card, usually by the end of the freshman year. Forty-one percent of these students carry an average balance of $584 and tend to spend an average of $131 a month.[20]

Generally, students must be eighteen years of age before they can apply for a card. Interest rates may be based on the student's income and whether the student has a job during school or is close to graduation.

For parents concerned that their children are not entirely ready to manage financial responsibility, two interesting options are available. The first is the prepaid card for which parents designate the amount of money to which the student has access. The second type of card is a traditional credit card that permits parents to set credit limits and track the account via a toll-free number or company Web site. College Parents of America, a national parents advocacy group, calls these two plans "cards with training wheels."

CREDIT CARD SEMINARS

As wary as students and parents should be of harassment by credit card companies, they should be equally wary of the credit card seminars the companies run in college communities. Despite the noble goals they state (such as showing students how credit cards work and the importance of maintaining credit worthiness), the credit card companies are in business to earn interest on your debt. In particular, students will want to beware of the credit card seminar dressed up as a fundraising event for a campus student group. Some credit card companies have cut deals with student groups whereby the group receives several dollars for each card application solicited at a seminar. No one gets something for nothing, and student groups owe it to their members to carefully scrutinize any business arrangement that translates into usurious interest rates on borrowed money.

The most common problem faced by students with credit cards is overextension. As students apply for and receive more cards, their spending further escalates along with their debt.

In a development that brings to mind the old adage "leaving the fox guarding the hen house," one major credit card company now runs advertising campaigns warning college students of the risks of carrying a heavy credit card debt and from misusing a credit card. While the company claims the advertising is designed to "raise consciousness among 18–24 year olds about the realities, importance, and implications of establishing a positive credit history through responsible credit card use," parents and students alike should be wary of a product that permits those without the resources or collateral to make a particular purchase, to make that purchase.

As credit card debt has become a big issue for college students, a growing number of schools have created programs to teach students about the risks of taking on high-interest credit card debt. According to an article by Todd Abrams for Student.Com, the majority of schools looking at the credit card issue are attempting a proactive approach. Instead of helping students who already owe creditors, schools are trying to help students keep themselves out of serious debt.

Interviewed for the on-line article, Linda Downing, the financial aid director at Rollins College in Winter Park, Florida, notes that she has seen the situation improve since Rollins began discussing credit card issues at freshman orientation. In particular, Downing is proud of the slightly different approach Rollins has taken, giving equal attention to educating parents as well as students. She adds, "Part of our focus is to make sure parents are aware that this is something that is going to happen to their children—that they will receive mail and solicitation that will give them opportunities to have credit cards."[21]

Campus bans on solicitation by credit card companies are increasingly common as well. As of this writing, Northeastern University and Tufts University in Massachusetts, Widener University in Pennsylvania, and Rollins College in Florida had all banned credit card companies from soliciting on their campuses.

THE BUDGET CRUNCH

Cramming, as common as it may be, just isn't healthy. So why do so many freshman students find themselves up late studying personal finance at some point during their first semester at college? They just didn't learn about it before they got to college. And this is where we, as parents, are often to blame. While there are many issues new college students are facing for the first time, money and budgeting should not be one of them. Do your son or daughter (and yourself) a favor by teaching him or her the basics of keeping a budget before any trouble happens. For this purpose and for those who like to think that way, nearly every student now has access to an Excel spreadsheet on his or her personal computer or at the campus computer lab. Reviewing with your child anticipated expenses—calculating liberally for pizza delivery—before classes start should be easy enough and may even provide some amusement for parents and students alike.

Bob Rollins, an elementary school teacher in Oakland, California, recalls one of his first eye-opening encounters with budgeting, as well as with cooking, when early in his sophomore year his turn came to do the food shopping for the apartment he shared with several others. Bob and another roommate went off to the market, only to return soon after, considerably poorer with several bags of food but nothing that even closely resembled breakfast, lunch, or dinner.[22]

If your son or daughter has never done the shopping on a budget for the family, this may be the time to start. While he or she is at it, maybe it's time junior did the cooking as well. If the meal is really hopeless, you can always be gracious at dinner and sneak a sandwich later after your now "experienced" cook and budget maven has gone up to his or her room for the night.

PROFESSIONAL ORGANIZERS

Professional organizers, for those who can afford one, are the place to go for help getting organized for college. Over time, they can also save you and your child money by teaching your child to properly budget for life while away at college. Diana Zimmerman, a busy professional organizer with a focus on parents and children, is a frequent lecturer and the author of a number of helpful brochures for parents on such issues as keeping in touch with a child away at college and packing the car for that first trip to college. Zimmerman's brochures for college students include one on roommates and another on setting up filing systems. Her Long Island, New York–based company, Solutions, runs seminars for parents on how to organize their lives. Zimmerman, who has also created a time line for parents with useful tips on college issues, is the author of many of the helpful hints on Bed, Bath, and Beyond's Web site—www.bedbathandbeyond.com— targeted at parents of college-bound children.[23]

Since paying for college isn't any fun, students and their parents should be sure to do all they can to take advantage of the financial breaks and payment plans many colleges make available. In addition to loans, financial aid, work study, and scholarships, students can pull their weight by being sure they make the most of their college experience. In this next chapter, I discuss things you and your son or daughter can do to be as academically prepared as possible for college and to make the most of these college years while on campus.

THREE

Choosing a Course of Study and Other Academic Concerns

■ ■ ■

WHO INFLUENCES YOUR CHILD?

The role of parents, if there is any, in helping their son or daughter choose a course of study varies greatly from family to family. For some families, college is a training ground where sons and daughters are expected to learn the rudiments of commerce before returning to a family-owned business. Most college students, however, plan for careers outside of the family business, often making the difficult calculation with incomplete or inaccurate information as to which field of study is a wise investment.

College students' views of the working world tend to be colored by the types of work their parents, siblings, and peers are engaged in, as well as by the industries that tend to economically dominate the region of the country from which they come. Also important is the student's aptitude for particular academic subjects. The significant influence of broader economic trends, the mass media, and guidance counselors figure in as well. For example, explosive growth in 2000 of dot-com start-up companies attracted many young people from all academic disciplines to computer science and business-related majors. Whether e-commerce will be enduring or fleeting, the explosion of Internet businesses has provided opportunities in other areas as well. With the Web driving a seemingly ceaseless demand for written content, for a while at least, many graduates with English or journalism majors were in demand as perhaps never before. Similarly, graphic designers experienced a boom in the job market as Web work expanded across all markets.

A student's choices about a course of study are also influenced by the income level or socioeconomic status of a student's family. More affluent parents who encourage their children to take a variety of courses and to explore a variety of fields may find that their children are less career-focused, at least initially, than students whose parents are hard-pressed to pay for college. Liberal arts majors may focus on courses that have nothing to do with work, only to later wish, upon entering the business world, that they had been more career-focused in their course selections. Gordon M. Henry, vice president for business development with i-Open.com, a Philadelphia dot-com start-up, majored in political science at Yale before shifting gears and deciding to pursue an MBA at Wharton. Henry notes the following:

> I wish I'd taken more practical business courses such as accounting as an undergraduate, not only to get the learning, but also to simply get the exposure to what running a business is all about. Despite the imposition of so-called "core curricula" in recent years, I think a fair number of liberal arts students still get away with taking courses that are interesting as opposed to ones that are truly useful.[1]

On the other hand, many students go the pre-med, pre-law, or pre-business route only to find it is not for them.

THE ROLE OF PART-TIME WORK

Given the difficulty some students experience in selecting the right major, part-time work may be the answer. As mentioned earlier, research shows that students who work part-time during college tend to perform somewhat better academically and focus sooner on a course of study than students who do not hold down jobs while in school. Interestingly, in Holland, where government stipends for university students have been reduced so that more than half of all Dutch students now hold down part-time jobs, students appear to be more focused on completing university as quickly as possible.[2]

POLITICAL INFLUENCES

The political climate of the country also has some effect on the courses of study students are pursuing. During the Vietnam War era, many U.S. students from politically conservative families found themselves pursuing courses of study and entertaining political and social attitudes that shocked their parents. The current emergence of a strong antisweatshop movement on college campuses and global protests against the International Monetary Fund are having a similar impact on a smaller group of college students. However, student political awareness and even activism should not cause parents alarm. Most young adults engage in a good deal of social experimentation and exploration of politics, and social action is generally not dangerous. As students move away from their families and begin to better define their own beliefs, pressures are inevitable. Just as a baby's fifth cold does not typically arouse the same level of parental concern as the first time a child becomes ill, by the time a child leaves for college, parents should be somewhat immunized against the views aired and comments their children may express. Most twenty-five- and thirty-year-olds no longer hold the same political views they held as freshmen and sophomores.

THE IMPORTANCE OF PARENT-CHILD DIALOGUE

So what can parents do to help their children select a course of study? Parents should seek a meaningful dialogue with their children about the classes they are choosing. In retrospect, my having taken a college class in ceramics was not tuition money well spent, and a conversation with my parents about my class selection might have helped. Even before the first class session, I had demonstrated a complete lack of aptitude for ceramics, and there were literally hundreds of other college classes that might have served me better. In the grander scheme of my life, this poor choice of class hours does not appear to have hurt me any, though neither did it help my intellectual development or application to graduate school. The contrary view, of course, is that college is precisely the time to take those classes you will not soon get to take again. I only wish I had chosen to explore another side of myself than that which drew me to ceramics.

While many parents will find their children reluctant to talk about classes, if done right, these conversations can benefit your child. Parents should not shrink from the challenge, as they often possess a superior, or at least more mature, appreciation of career goals and the importance of a good undergraduate education in getting there. A simple "Why have you chosen those classes?" voiced in a non-accusatory tone encourages a child to explain his or her motivations and expectations of the semester. As with many other aspects of the post-high-school parent-child relationship, parents will be assisting their children when they demonstrate some backbone on issues that matter in the long term, such as courses of study.

For most students, choosing a course of study should not be as daunting a task as it may at first seem. Parents can contribute to the decision-making process by helping their children identify or recall their strong academic suits. Parents can also encourage their children to consider *who* is teaching the class, not just *what* the subject matter is. Sometimes, for instance, colleges rightfully boast about "star" professors or about the quality of a particular academic department. Parents who know of a particular professor's reputation for fine teaching may want to let their son or daughter in on the secret and gently urge them to consider taking a class with the well-regarded teacher.

HELPING YOUR SON OR DAUGHTER MAP OUT AN ACADEMIC PLAN

Parents, particularly those who have gone to college themselves, can help make their children aware of the importance of careful academic planning. Regrettably, many students arrive at school thinking they are prepared for the work, only to find themselves struggling with the competing demands of classes and social life. Many students also find they have a hard time adjusting to the lack of parental supervision and the lack of routine that often goes hand-in-hand with living apart from one's family. Falling behind academically may have drastic effects, particularly for those who may have received an academic scholarship.

Dr. Deborah Hahn, assistant dean for undergraduate academic affairs at Brandeis University in Waltham, Massachusetts, stresses the importance of careful academic planning during the college years so that students do not lose their hard-earned grants. For example, many students are surprised to find themselves struggling to meet minimum GPA requirements set by scholarship committees. Dr. Hahn gives the following advice:

> I urge parents with whom I speak to advise their son or daughter to make an appointment with the dean or an academic counselor during the phase of the semester when they are finalizing their course selections. Students who have put so much time and effort into researching and winning scholarships are well equipped for success in college, but they would be well served to use the same careful strategies once they arrive.[3]

But parents and students alike need to accept that college preparation really needs to start much earlier, in high school at the latest. Start early and keep with it. John Katzman runs the Princeton Review, a test preparation and counseling company. According to him, college-bound high school students should take four years of challenging courses. At best, the last two years should include honors and advanced placement (AP) courses. At least, they should include the "four solids" (math, English, science, and history) every year. Colleges care more about course selection than grades: they want evidence that the student will accept challenge and succeed. Since weak elementary and middle school math skills can make algebra and geometry tougher, and make the SAT a nightmare, Katzman suggests special effort to address those problems as early as possible. Tutoring should address the underlying problems in fractions and percentages before it aims at the high school curriculum.

Katzman adds that in addition to helping students pay their bills, parents can help their children once they have left for college by refusing to accept excuses for poor academic performance. He suggests that parents tie a student's spending money to the child's taking a reasonable number of courses and getting minimally acceptable grades (perhaps a 3.0 average). There are few students who can really go wild in college and maintain a solid GPA.[4]

ACADEMIC READINESS

Helping your child prepare for college should include some focus on organization, study habits, and time management. If nothing else, parents can help out by purchasing an easy-to-use database software package and extra memory for their child's computer. A good file cabinet (cardboard file boxes will do) and a short lesson in paper records management will help as well. Unless your child is a speed reader with a photographic memory, he or she will find that the first year of college means a great deal of reading and writing. Those majoring in the liberal arts will especially find this to be the case.

As someone whose handwriting is beyond atrocious, I will forever mourn the fact that laptops were neither affordable nor widely available when I went to college. Today, along with PalmPilots, cell phones, and portable MP3 music players, laptops are de rigueur in the college classroom. While I am generally not fond of the proliferation of the electronic gadgetry, I feel every student should own a laptop. If you can afford to purchase one for your child, substitute this for the desktop PC or Mac purchase you might have budgeted for. Your child can get used to the smaller keyboard and will be forever grateful for the fact that she or he can carry the device into class. Remind your child to mind her or his belongings, as laptops and other small electronic devices are prime targets of campus thieves. (Chapter 7 discusses campus safety issues including theft.)

Okay, so now you have spent the money and purchased the stuff. What about helping your child actually prepare for the work? Well, apart from moving in with your child at college and frequent e-mail messages, your involvement should be limited to just that— preparation. In an interview with me in February 2001, Kenneth Breuer, Ph.D., a professor of engineering at Brown University, expressed concern that some of his students do not have enough background or intellectual stamina to complete the rigors of an engineering curriculum:

> The standard complaint I have as a scientist is that college students today do not have as strong a basis in the fundamentals of math and physics as they once had, and so those parts of the college curriculum are harder than they used to be. You can teach almost any aspect of science to a student with a good foundation.[5]

Another challenge for a professor in the hard sciences is that one likes to see students who, when faced with difficult concepts, are prepared to work independently to conquer the subject. Instead, complain professors in the sciences, many of today's college students want to be fed what they need to know. According to Dr. Breuer, "The system discourages students from taking the initiative and going it alone." That said, for the most part, teaching engineering students is a pleasure for Dr. Breuer, and he says there are few greater rewards than seeing that light go on in the heads of students who are engaged by their work.

For another perspective, I spoke with Anne Foster, Ph.D., a history professor at Saint Anselm College in Manchester, New Hampshire. Dr. Foster has found students generally well prepared for college work:

> Contrary to what parents might think, based on my own experience and listening to college faculty talking around their version of the water cooler, I hear that most students are competently prepared to handle the academic work at their college or university. They know how to write sentences, paragraphs,

and essays. They know how to extract information from a lecture or assigned reading. They often even know how to formulate a basic response to the argument of a text.[6]

But parents should be worried if their children are not learning these skills in high school. Dr. Foster has also found students lacking in such skills as doing independent research, constructing logical, thought-out arguments and sustaining them through an essay, and knowing how to analytically compare different arguments made by different authors. She assumes, however, that it is her job to help them acquire these skills while they are in college. Students should be prepared to learn new ways of learning once they go to college.

PLAGIARISM

Parents need to get wise to what their college-bound children have known for years: the Internet has facilitated an explosion in the amount of cheating by college students.

"Virtual Fake Outs—Where Have You Seen That Paper Before? Uh, Probably Online" is the title of a well-written if disturbing article by Hervey Pean for Student.Com, a Web site targeting the college market. The article cites 1998 statistics reporting that cheating at Virginia Tech increased from 80 incidents in 1995–1996 to 280 incidents during the 1996–1997 school year. And, in 1997, out of concern over the growing problem of plagiarism, Boston University filed a federal lawsuit against on-line term paper mills. Pean goes on to say the following:

> Plagiarism used to require a significant amount of effort. Students would have to do substantial research at a library, or re-use a friend's work. But now just performing a keyword search on your desired topic can get you all you need for an A+ paper. A person can select the text they want, cut and paste it and submit it as their own work.[7]

I spoke as well with Dr. Foster of Saint Anselm College about the problem of plagiarism. She notes that academic dishonesty seems to be endemic:

> I would characterize student attitudes toward plagiarism as follows: first, they are ignorant of what constitutes academic dishonesty and plagiarism, and second, they are making no effort to inform themselves. . . . I think few students come to such a sense of ownership about their own words and so never care about the words and thoughts of others.[8]

This is, therefore, another place where parents should be involved. Parents should not shrink from the opportunity and obligation to teach their son or daughter that plagiarism and cheating are part of a continuum of unacceptable dishonesty. Defending it in one's mind as a means of getting where you want to go is "twisted," to use a word students use to describe troubled classmates.

Another attitude that many professors observe among students who cheat or plagiarize is the thinking that, if they can get away with it, then it is fine. And it is so much easier for them to get away with academic dishonesty and outright plagiarism these days, mostly because of the Internet. The sources at their disposal are too vast for professors to check. Even when she started teaching, some years ago at the State University of New York at Cortland, Dr. Foster could assume that her students had done research for their papers either in the Cortland or the nearby Cornell University libraries. From time to time, she would find a handful of plagiarized papers by looking for likely sources in those libraries. Now, if professors suspect that someone other than the student has written the paper, they could never check all of the probable sources for that paper. And students know that and know that professors are busy people, unlikely to take the time to check. This has led some professors to design assignments that are difficult to plagiarize, though not all professors exercise this precaution.

Many students appear misinformed about what plagiarism actually is. The Modern Language Association (MLA) defines plagiarism as passing off another person's work as his or her own. Plagiarism, according to the MLA, includes using a person's words, ideas, and concepts and paraphrasing material without citing the original source. *Plagiarism does not only mean copying someone's work word-for-word.*[9]

Parents can help out by teaching their children what plagiarism is and by teaching them good study habits so they do not feel the temptation to cheat. And, as William DeJong, Ph.D., professor of health communications at Boston University and director of the Higher Education Center notes, some students may be deterred by knowing that a college's penalties for plagiarism are usually severe, ranging from a failing grade in the course to expulsion from the university.[10]

Of course, students who cheat, or perhaps students in general, tend to be lazy. An easy way for professors to catch at least some of those who plagiarize is to look at the first five to ten hits that come up on a good Web search engine query. Additionally, several start-up software companies and a number of university researchers are racing to develop software that would quickly identify material that has been taken from the Web. Parents can help their children resist the temptation to cheat or plagiarize by pointing out the increasing probability that they will be caught doing so. Parents may also want to remind their son or daughter that in a growing number of states, paper mills, which charge students for term papers, are illegal. While no one likes to resort to threats, particularly with their children, deterrence often works and deserves support as a cheating prevention strategy.

EVALUATING THE TEACHING AT A SCHOOL

Another way for parents and college students to gauge a school's commitment to teaching and learning is to consider schools that have encouraged student evaluations of professors and then make that information publicly available. Unfortunately, few colleges have made it easy to obtain such information, though a campus newspaper (increasingly available on-line) may be a good place to begin your search.

FOUR

Living the Student Life

◧   ◧   ◧

This chapter discusses how parents may be able to help their college-bound son or daughter prepare for and adjust to the social scene at college. It also explores athletics, sexual orientation, accommodation of students with disabilities, issues of race and ethnicity, and faith issues. Let's start with the roommate issues. For many, living with new roommates is one of the hardest adjustments to make.

THE IMPORTANCE OF THE HOUSING QUESTIONNAIRE

A thirty-something friend in Boston describes his first year away from home this way:

> I left the security of my home in suburban Fairfield County, Connecticut, for college early, at seventeen, after my junior year in high school. High school was not really working out for me, so I took a year at a small arty school in Greenwich Village in New York City.
>
> When I arrived at my apartment on move-in day, everyone was very friendly and helped me out with my suitcases, boxes, and stereo. Once I'd settled into my room, one of my new roommates looked me over for a while before saying, "So you're my new roommate. I guess you didn't read the housing questionnaire?" Surprised by his comment, I looked up and asked him why he'd said that. It turns out I'd been placed in

an all gay suite, with a group who liked to stay out much of the night partying. The situation worked out fine, though I did transfer after a term to an apartment more in keeping with my [straight] lifestyle.[1]

Study habits, smoking, musical taste, night owl versus early riser, fitness nut, party animal, and slob; these are just some of the things that parents and their college-bound sons or daughters should consider and include when filling out the questionnaire. I still remember the sweet odor of marijuana wafting out of a neighboring dorm room in my freshman dorm and still can see the dog-eared stacks of hard core porn my roommate couldn't seem to pull himself away from except during exam period. Surely this was not the focused, intellectual roommate my parents and I had hoped for when filling out my housing questionnaire.

With students coming to college from an increasingly diverse cultural and social pool, issues like diet and religious and cultural beliefs may be parts of the housing questionnaire that your son or daughter will want to pay particularly close attention to. While some students may feel most comfortable living with another student of the same religious, ethnic, or racial group, others will want to use the housing experience to get to know a student who comes from another background altogether. Still other students may want, or not want, to room with athletes, while many will express no preference one way or the other. Finally, the colleges themselves often have their own ideas about the role of housing in fostering a sense of community on campus. This philosophy may mean pairing up roommates who, on the face of it, appear quite different from one another.

To help with the integration of different students into residence halls and classes, many colleges have created student affairs offices focused on diversity issues. In principle, the programs run by these offices help students adjust to college life with students who may be very different from them in outlook, heritage, and beliefs. University-supported Asian American, African American, Latino, international, and gay and lesbian students associations are other ways in which colleges help students of different backgrounds adjust to campus life.

CONFLICTS WITH ROOMMATES

Visualize this: your son's or daughter's new roommate will probably be just as nervous about the new living arrangement as your son or daughter will be. No matter how carefully a student completes the housing questionnaire, chances are there will be some surprises once he or she gets to school. Maybe the roommate(s) did not answer truthfully or the housing office misplaced the questionnaires and ended up picking roommates out of a hat. Chances are, even if the housing office worked long and hard at matching applicants (most do), one in four new students will still feel he or she has drawn his or her worst nightmare as a roommate. Do not panic. If things are really that bad, a student can usually seek a housing transfer.

According to Kit Williams, the former associate director of residential life at Boston University, roommate problems are one of the biggest issues for first-year students and parents.[2] Almost everyone has at least one roommate conflict, and most have many. It is just the result of living with others in close quarters, and for many students, it is the first time they are sharing a room, often a small room. Some college and university residence halls have freshmen living together in triples and quads.

Although some students will want to live with an old friend, parents may want to advise their college-bound student to be wary of rooming with a friend from home. Williams has the following to say about this:

> I have seen lots of the "best friends from home" deciding to room together and having it ruin relationships. Often it turns out that old friends do not really know how their best friends live—their habits for getting up, going to sleep, how they do homework (e.g., with TV and stereo on or in relative silence), sharing issues, food issues, guest issues, smoking, etc.[3]

At many colleges, roommate brochures or roommate bills of rights can help roommates, be they old friends or strangers, sort through these issues.

Another sensitive area, explains Williams, is when, if ever, parents should intervene in roommate conflicts.[4] These situations tend to be difficult because parents are sometimes far away from their child for the first time, want to help, and are often footing a big tuition bill. Having a child call home all upset about a roommate issue is a challenge—and some parents want it fixed right away by some outside force. If there is a miscommunication between roommates with no serious problems, such as infractions of the law or school policy, and a student's safety is not at risk, it generally works best to have the roommates try to work it out alone. If that does not work, the students may want to bring the conflict to the attention of the resident assistant (RA), or, if necessary, to the resident director (RD). According to Williams, "It was rare in my experience that a roommate was moved out of a room in cases where there were not serious problems. It was always our goal to try to assist the students in their problem solving to become better roommates."[5]

However, if there is a serious issue in a room, such as one roommate threatening another or a roommate having a gun in violation of the school policy, the concerned roommate should go to the RA or some other authority, or a notified parent should promptly call the school. A student in possession of a dangerous weapon or threats by one student against another underscore the importance of colleges providing parents with information on whom to call if there is a problem. Particularly when threats of physical harm or weapons are involved, parents should be able to contact the right authority at the campus immediately. Little is more frustrating for parents than getting referred from one person to another during anxious periods such as this.

In the past, phone bills were a sticky roommate issue. In recent years, however, the problem appears to have abated since students have been given their own phones or a long distance access number. At schools where joint phone billing may still be an issue, parents may want their son or daughter to get a long distance calling card or a cell phone of his or her own. Many students already have one.

WHAT TO BRING TO COLLEGE

Williams offers the following advice to parents and students on setting up a dorm room:

- It is often good to consult with a roommate so students do not end up having too much stuff in their room. Provided all roommates are amenable to sharing, it works to "divide and conquer" when it comes to things like televisions, stereos, microwave ovens, microfridges, and toaster ovens.
- Since space is often an issue, some students have opted to either raise their beds (for storage underneath) or loft them. It is a good idea to check dorm guidelines in advance of construction. This way the student will not end up building something only to find out he or she cannot take it into the dorm or has to tear down the structure that he or she has built. The lofts that do best are sturdily built and provide enough clearance so that a person can sit up in bed on the loft without hitting the light fixtures or ceiling.
- Check in advance just what sort of things the school supplies. Some colleges, for example, supply bulletin boards in the rooms. Other schools have strict guidelines about what one can put up on the walls (e.g., no nails in the walls). For students living in the popular cinderblock high-rises that so many colleges built during the 1960s, there are great cinderblock hooks you can buy that will hold up most anything.[6]

Other items students may want to bring to school include the following:

- a wastebasket for the room
- a flashlight and batteries (for power outages)
- a pair of flip-flops to wear into the shower
- a shower pail for carrying shampoo, toothbrush, and other toiletries into the bathroom

- a good lamp (often residence hall lighting is fluorescent and some students prefer incandescent)
- a soft rug for near the bed (often there are industrial grade carpets on the dorm room floor, so a nice rug can give a room a homey touch)

For those colleges and universities that are not yet offering the ID/debit card that does everything, a mountain of quarters is important (for laundry, parking, soda machines, and so on).

The tendency of college students to cram their rooms full of too much stuff is a real problem both for students and for many colleges. Moving in, which used to be a few quick trips up and down the flights of dorm stairs can now take many hours. Hey, at least your son's or daughter's Razor scooter is collapsible. Does he or she really need all that stuff? Of course not, but how do you tell him or her that? Maybe the answer is to make sure the SUV is in the shop the week you are scheduled to leave for school. Better yet, sell the SUV and buy a fuel-efficient compact with a tiny gas tank and trunk or hatchback to match. Then make your point by telling your son or daughter that as much stuff as fits in the car is all you can carry.

Electronics are creating another problem for colleges. At my alma mater, Michigan, the wattage has simply not kept pace with the students' heavy demands for electricity for computers, boom boxes, and PalmPilots. Electrical blackouts and increased fire risks are now on the knowledgeable college residence hall directors' radar screens along with beer kegs and theft of furniture from common areas.

While you are likely to lose many of the battles over what to take to school, try and make sure that at least a few pens and notebooks make it into the packing. After all, students can't take class notes with a microwave oven.

DORM ROOMS AND FIRE SAFETY

Parental concerns about dorm room safety are sometimes warranted. Many college residence halls are outdated structures with inadequate exits, emergency exit signs, and sprinkler systems. Dormitory renovations are costly, and sometimes public code inspectors and college risk managers have not kept up with the latest in fire safety and dorm security. The fatal fire during the winter of 2000 at Seton Hall University in New Jersey has prompted congressional activity, as well as greatly heightened awareness among informed parents of the mixed record of colleges and universities with fire safety.

Under a bill unanimously approved in June 2000 by the U.S. House of Representatives, colleges would be required to provide statistics to students and their parents on the occurrence of fires and false alarms in each of their dormitories, including information on deaths and injuries that have resulted from fires in the two preceding years. Although reporting requirements alone will not make college residence halls any safer, legislation of this sort can be expected to move colleges to conduct thorough reviews of their fire safety and emergency procedures.

Parents and students concerned about dormitory conditions and safety should carefully consider the dorm or house in which the student will be spending much of his or her first year of college. Although I was less conscious of dorm conditions as a student, as a parent it never ceases to amaze me what some colleges have the chutzpah to call "housing."

Although there has been much in the Boston and national media these past few years about all the things colleges are doing to improve dorm life, many schools still rest on their academic laurels, legacy, and location to avoid addressing basic lack of habitability issues that no private landlord in a medium to large city would get away with. In my experience, most college housing options are adequate, with some exceptionally good and others poor. Parents who care about such things may be amazed to find that some of the Ivy League schools are among the worst offenders. Sure, these schools tend to offer excellent Web access in dorm rooms, but there may also be more students per room than one would find in a comparable hotel room on spring break in Cancun. Given the tuition bills all of you are soon to be or are already facing, something is wrong with this picture.

COLLEGE PARENT GUIDES

To their credit, more and more colleges are now creating short parent brochures and newsletters designed to answer some of the questions parents may have about college life. Roommate matters and other issues related to student social life are common themes of these college guides for parents. Cornell University's parents' guide, one of the better brochures I have seen, includes a letter from the dean of students and sections that cover the following:

- what's ahead
- academic advising
- choosing or changing majors
- changing colleges within Cornell
- grade reports
- money matters
- health, safety, and human relations
- student life
- staying in touch
- ways to get involved
- other resources
- a list of important telephone numbers[7]

Separation, drinking and drug use, and campus safety are other common themes of these often-useful guides for parents.

COLLEGE EXPERIENCE PROGRAMS

Though typically not designed to help parents make the adjustment to a son or daughter going away to college, many colleges now offer excellent college experience programs for high school students that may be helpful to parents as well. These programs may be a good way for high school students and parents to get a feel for college life before leaving for college. High school students enrolled in these summer programs tend to live in the dormitories and attend classes in regular college classroom buildings. While these programs tend to be well supervised and highly structured, high school student participants may actually get a glimpse of undergraduate life during their stay on campus. For those who can afford to attend the programs, which range from academically rigorous to empty padding for a college application, the benefits to both parents and students can be real.

GREEK LIFE

So what are those houses with the funny letters on the front and beer cans littering the lawn? To the uninitiated, the rituals of Greek life and particularly "rush" will come as something of a shock. Fraternities and sororities are a common feature of many, though not all, college campuses. While a diverse lot in their own right, in general, these social and service organizations tend to recruit members through a process known as rush. Traditionally, this intense period of recruiting involves freshmen and sophomore students making the rounds of fraternity or sorority events at which the men are greeted with the traditional, "I'm Bob; damn glad to meet you," and women, "Hi, I'm Candace; it's good to meet you." While very much under fire in recent years for their bad boy and libertine ways, fraternities and sororities are alive and thriving on many campuses. Concerns and accusations that Greek life sometimes promotes hazing, sexual harassment, out-of-control student drinking, and racial and ethnic bigotry have fallen on deaf ears among many young college students. Given the deserved bad reputation of some of the chapters, as they are known, reading up on Greek life before becoming a pledge is a wise strategy.

Deferred Rush

If a student is set on going Greek, parents and students should find out whether the college the student plans to attend subscribes to a deferred rush policy. For years, colleges have toyed with the idea of deferring Greek rush until later in the school year. For example, in May 2000, Richard Mullendore, the University of Georgia's vice president for student affairs, announced that he would push for delaying rush until spring semester.[8] Vice President Mullendore's comments came at a Greek summit held six weeks after an Alpha Tau Omega member died in a car wreck during a fraternity event involving fifteen students. Four men associated with the fraternity have been indicted on charges of vehicular homicide and involuntary manslaughter in the case.

According to Vice President Mullendore, the strategy of deferring rush until students get settled into their classes and develop a routine will help "improve fraternity and sorority life."[9] Perhaps "preserve life" would have been a more candid choice of words. Sue Kraft Fussell, executive director of the Association of Fraternity Advisors in Indianapolis, notes that although fraternity and sorority recruitment usually takes place within the first few weeks or months after students arrive at college, deferred rush is becoming more common across the country.[10]

Reasons Students Join

The North-American Interfraternity Conference has created *A Parent's Guide to Fraternities—How Can Your Son Benefit from Fraternity Membership?* The brochure states the following:

> For your son, making the transition from high school or a community college to a four-year college or university may seem like an imposing challenge. One or more of the following questions may be on his mind:
>
> - Will I fit in and make new friends?
> - Will I be able to succeed academically?
> - Will I be able to get involved in campus organizations and better my leadership skills?
> - Will I find other people interested in the same things that I am?

- How can I prepare for my career?
- Will I feel like a part of the campus community or just another number?[11]

According to the North-American Interfraternity Conference, fraternities exist as a proven support network for young men as they embark on this new period in their lives.[12] Over 400,000 students across the country are currently fraternity members. Fraternities, the conference argues, can help personalize your son's college experience by offering a scholastic support system; hands-on experience in leading committees, managing budgets, and interacting with faculty and administrators; exposure to potential careers through educational programs and discussions with alumni; and the chance to give back to the community through service projects. Other benefits are the close friendships and support some members find in Greek life.

The Struggle to Limit Greek Activity

Greek alumni resistance to the widespread assault on fraternities and sororities as a source of out-of-control drinking is quite strong nationally and with respect to Greek life on particular campuses. In April 2000, Dartmouth College announced a plan for controlling problems at its Greek houses that is a far cry from the aggressive Greek ban it had proposed earlier. According to an April 21, 2000, article in the *Boston Globe,*

> [in its action] the Dartmouth board of trustees retreated from initial proposals that could have eliminated the so-called Greek system. As a result, Dartmouth fraternity and sorority leaders are breathing a sigh of relief, even though the new policy could spell the end of their signature keg parties. "The campus exploded . . . when the recommendations first came out," said Jaimie A. Paul, former president of the Coed Fraternity Sorority Council. "We thought the Greek system was going to be eliminated. This is definitely a leap from where we are now, but it's not as huge as we thought it was going to be."[13]

Nonetheless, the plan will reportedly implement sweeping changes in all areas of student life, from the removal of taps and bars in fraternities to redesigned dormitories.

The *Globe* article describes how Dartmouth's Student Life Initiative has been evolving since February 1999. The final plan "restricts the ability of Greek organizations to attract students, hold raucous parties, or force their pledges to endure the ritual indignations of hazing."[14] But the plan is clearly a retreat from a recommendation that only seniors and juniors who are Greek officers should be allowed to live in residential sororities and fraternities on campus. Moreover, the plan seems to have been stream-rolled forward even though faculty voted 81–0 earlier in the year in favor of Dartmouth withdrawing recognition of the Greek system.

To parents concerned that their son or daughter select a college or university that promotes a healthy lifestyle and builds individual responsibility and character, the interest of Dartmouth's admissions office in the school's action against Greek organizations is especially noteworthy. According to the *Globe* article,

> Admissions officers at Dartmouth had long feared that the school was failing to attract many of the highest-caliber students because of its reputation as a school primarily made up of beer-guzzling white males.
>
> In a survey of those accepted to the class of 2003, many students who decided not to attend Dartmouth cited their concerns about social life as their primary reason to go elsewhere. They tended to be the best students, with the highest SAT scores.[15]

Just as many parents are not familiar with the realities of campus social life, college trustees at many schools are often not aware of the ways Greek life sometimes contributes to hazing, sexual harassment, out-of-control student drinking, and racial and ethnic bigotry. With this in mind, I hope you will buy copies of this book to send to trustees at your alma mater as well as at the school selected by your son or daughter.

Dartmouth's struggle to change its Greek culture is indicative of the uphill battle faced by the college and others like it in confronting entrenched attitudes about high-risk drinking. According to Dartmouth's dean of student life, Holly Sateia, "The appeal of a party in the basement of a fraternity is it's like a party where the student's parents aren't home. If colleges want to compete with that we're going to have to give the students more of a social option [than we're currently giving them]."[16]

Hazing

A spring 2000 e-mail from the Higher Education Center for Alcohol and Other Drug Prevention reads as follows:

1. Six Theta Chi fraternity members at the University of North Texas have been arrested, and their chapter has been temporarily suspended from campus after allegations of alcohol-related hazing offenses.
2. More on the University of Georgia fraternity member that died in a car accident in an incident related to rush activities.
3. A hockey team member is the second student to be criminally charged for the alleged hazing of underclassmen at the University of Vermont.
4. A North Carolina State University student was shot early Sunday while he struggled with a would-be robber on the front porch of a fraternity house.[17]

Despite newly enacted antihazing legislation in many states, the practice of hazing goes on in various forms throughout the country. According to author Hank Nuwer, alcohol misuse and hazing cannot be eliminated, but it can be controlled. In his 1999 book, *Wrongs of Passage: Fraternities, Sororities, Hazing, and Binge Drinking,* Nuwer says the following:

Hazers are in effect extremists. They justify actions that are outside the range of normal human behavior. People join extremist groups because they crave relationships and acceptance, not primarily because they respond to the group's particular ideology. . . . Fraternities and sororities "rush" predominantly first-year male and female college students who find themselves in unfamiliar settings, away from family and from childhood friends, and who seek a feeling of belonging. Part of the exhilaration some college students experience upon their arrival in college involves their ability to choose a Greek group that offers them friendships, some that are quite likely to endure for life. To these young people, enduring hazing beats the pain of loneliness.[18]

While some readers may feel that it is Nuwer himself who is the extremist, what can parents tell their son or daughter about hazing that will keep them from falling victim to it, or, as a bystander, permitting it to occur? There are several things. First, as noted above, hazing is illegal in many states. Even where it is not, however, it is widely barred by college conduct policy. Additionally, any activity that puts one at risk of death or serious bodily injury, such as forcing someone to drink twenty-one shots of alcohol, can generally be prosecuted criminally.

Though the practice is barred at many schools, hazing still goes on behind closed, and sometimes not-so-closed, doors. Parents should be sensitive to their son's or daughter's fear of social stigmatization that might occur for reporting a hazing incident, but students should be encouraged to report such incidents to campus law enforcement and to the dean of student life. These matters need to be treated seriously, and if they know what is good for them, campus police and administrators will respond appropriately. In recent years, many colleges and administrators who have not meaningfully responded to allegations and evidence of hazing have ended up on the front page of the newspaper and on national television. Nothing is more damaging to a school than an allegation that it has been light on a criminal activity.

ATHLETICS

One particularly insightful observation about college athletics was offered to me in June 2000 by Karl Lindholm, the dean of advising at Middlebury College in Vermont. Dean Lindholm warns that many schools are "failing to assimilate their athletes into the general student population."[19] Given their rigorous practice and workout schedules and their focus on sports rather than academics, many athletes fall behind in their studies. As these athletes develop feelings of inadequacy about their academic work, many are driven further into a focus on athletics and further away from the classroom.

An added stress on college athletes at schools with competitive athletic programs can be the gambling that has become commonplace in college sports. Although forty-nine states have laws against betting on college athletics (as of this writing, it was still legal to bet on college sports in Nevada), the practice is widespread among fans and some players. The pressure on some athletes to take into account a big game's point spread is very real, prompting the National Collegiate Athletic Association (NCAA) and many coaches to support a total ban on betting on college athletics. The undue pressure on young college athletes to shave points off a game is not what college athletics was meant to be.

SEXUAL ORIENTATION

Whatever your own lifestyle or sexual orientation, as parents, get ready for a new view of sexuality and gender at college. At most public and private colleges—including many nominally religiously affiliated schools—gay, lesbian, bisexual, and transgender student groups are flourishing, and gay students, faculty, and staff no longer have to hide their lifestyle choices from the public. In October 2000, the University of Pennsylvania accepted a $2 million gift from a gay couple who met as undergraduates at Penn. In making their donation, the couple acknowledged how, as early as 1982 when they were students there, Penn had taken a leadership role on gay issues, acknowledging the issues that gay and lesbian students face and providing services for them. Their generous donation will be used to renovate a gay and lesbian student center at the university.

Even at colleges with firmly religious affiliations, more and more students are finding the courage to come out. Gay unions (weddings) in campus chapels are increasingly commonplace and, as if a confirmation of the growing number of gays in society at large, Vermont has become the first state in the nation to publicly recognize gay unions by authorizing town clerks to perform marriages.

For some parents, the mere existence of this subsection will make them uncomfortable. Whether for religious or cultural reasons, or for reasons of plain old bigotry, some people continue to deny that homosexuality is anything but an abomination. But despite these negative attitudes, gay student life on campus is thriving and here to stay. Even the book titles and newly created positions at some universities attest to the explosive growth in the number of students who are coming out in college. *Working with Lesbian, Gay, Bisexual, and Transgender College Students—A Handbook for Faculty and Administrators*, a 1998 book from Greenwood Press, is a reference work for faculty, deans, and other student life administrators. Although not all parents are happy about it, lesbian and gay students now constitute a significant percentage of students on most college campuses. Indeed, on a few campuses, the number of gay students may even rival the percentage of straight students. Whatever the breakdown, more and more students are coming to college having already come out, and many others are discovering their sexual orientation while at school.

Whatever personal prejudices you may have about homosexuality—we all have prejudices about something or another—it is essential that, as parents, you accept just how difficult it is to provide needed attention to gay and lesbian students' needs if administrators, and other parents, do not understand the issues or how to address them. As more faculty and administrators, especially those who may struggle personally with understanding the gay lifestyle, become familiar with the issues gay students face, services to lesbian and gay students can be expected to improve. Parents whose child has come out in high school or during college may wish to seek out other parents or groups of parents who have gone through similar experiences. Learning how others have come to terms with a child's lifestyle that is different from your own may help you to maintain a close relationship with a gay son or lesbian daughter. Just as all parents seek a safe and welcoming environment for their college-bound child, parents of gay or lesbian college students should do all they can to ensure that the college their child is attending is as accepting of their child's lifestyle as it is of other students' at the school.

Supportive faculty and staff often play an important role in helping gay and lesbian students overcome obstacles that their lifestyle may have thrown in the way of their academic and professional development. For some gay students with family members who refuse to accept their homosexuality, college may represent a protected place where the students can be themselves without suffering verbal abuse or physical harm. Often, at least in the first decade of the new millennium, gay and lesbian students may still feel stigmatized by their families and their communities. Parents can help their children by being as understanding as they can about their child's lifestyle, even if it is something they do not entirely understand.

Some of the issues that gay or lesbian students, and ultimately their parents, face include

- finding a college that offers gay and lesbian students good institutional and emotional support
- depression and stress
- discrimination and hate crime activity
- residence life issues
- career planning
- health and counseling issues including HIV/AIDS
- same-sex dating and domestic violence
- issues related to athletics and Greek life

HISTORICALLY BLACK COLLEGES AND UNIVERSITIES AND NATIVE AMERICAN TRIBAL COLLEGES

The goals of this section are quite modest—to present some resources parents and students of color may want to consider when applying for college. As noted in chapter 1, colleges, today and in the future, will be more diverse racially and culturally than at any other time in history.

Many colleges today have a diversity coordinator, and many schools have administrative offices of minority affairs. Additionally, parents of all races and ethnicities may want their sons and daughters to consider some of the exceptional public and private historically black colleges and universities and Native American tribal colleges that exist across the country.

I have no interest in becoming embroiled in the thorny question of race-based theme houses and whether they foster or help combat educational inequality in higher education. The core issue for parents and students, whatever their race, ethnicity, or national origin is what sort of school is best for the student? Is a fine historically black college or university like Spelman College or Howard University the place for my son or daughter, or would he or she do better at another kind of college? Janelle Farris, a Spelman graduate from Seattle, found historically black Spelman in Atlanta the type of school that permitted her to thrive both socially and academically. Having grown up in a city with a relatively small African American community, she found it important that she attend a college that cherishes and fosters her cultural heritage. She also recalls Spelman offering her a comfort level she does not believe she would have found at a small, mostly white New England college.[20]

Spelman College is one of four schools that make up the Atlanta University Center. Students are able to take classes at any one of the four Center schools—Morris Brown, Clark Atlanta University, Spelman, and Morehouse. So, although Spelman is a school for women, classes are typically coeducational, and the atmosphere is not gender-segregated. The schools are lively, the campuses are beautiful, and each of them is growing in national prominence.

With racial and ethnic segregation a fact of life on college campuses nationally and campus hate crimes directed at racial and ethnic minorities a growing problem, students of color who have the luxury of doing so should seek out a college that is as welcoming as possible. College is hard enough without the intrusion of societal racism and criminal bias. On the campus tour and in reviewing college materials, parents of students of color should pay careful attention to the language used by students, admissions officers, faculty, and the college brochures in addressing issues of race and ethnicity. When visiting a campus, preferably when school is in session, observe the way students of different races and ethnicities appear to interact with one another. Read the school and community newspaper, and do your research. Parents should also ask hard questions of deans, students, and others about the campus environment. At some urban campuses located in largely minority communities, minority students have been known to complain about being stopped by campus police just because they are of color. Even at small rural colleges, in recent years there have been several incidents in which an African American student was falsely accused by campus or local police of some criminal offense or another. Such events can undo in a short time the major strides a campus has made in creating a more tolerant or welcoming environment.

Janelle Farris explains her choice of Spelman as follows:

> Growing up in Seattle, I was frequently the only African American in my class. The comments and questions that my grade school classmates innocently and not-so-innocently asked were the stuff of difference; they were the root of my understanding that being black made me something "other" and that "other" was not necessarily a good thing in white society. "How come your braids move like that? Do you wear hair spray?" and "Why did God make you black?" are just a couple examples of my early childhood education.

High school brought new challenges. Having been the only black for so many of my early years, I was now too "white" for my "brothers and sisters" and too black for the white students. Dating was not something that came easily; a basketball playing tomboy, I was uncomfortable with racial lines drawn without my understanding and uncomfortable with myself in the flirty world of teenaged girls.

I chose to go to Spelman because I thought it would be a place where skin color wouldn't be an issue. In a place where everyone is black, I could be free to learn about myself and make friends without unwritten rules about racial divides that I did not understand. That thought turned out to be my reality in the black oasis I found in Atlanta. Although I admit that there were other color lines to learn and try to understand— bright skinned versus dark—I mostly avoided that challenging divide and found a home within myself and in my school.[21]

Regarding the social scene at Spelman and other historically black colleges and universities, parents should know that as at any American university, drinking, drug use, and parties are a part of the experience. That said, the research suggests that student alcohol and drug use at both public and private historically black colleges and universities tends to be lower than drinking and drug use in the college student population overall.[22]

As far as academics and teaching, many of the Native American tribal colleges and the nation's public and private historically black colleges and universities are special places where faculty take a profound interest in all of the students, including those who show only a limited desire to succeed academically. According to Janelle Farris, who graduated from Spelman with honors and later earned a master's degree from Harvard's John F. Kennedy School of Government:

> I graduated from college a woman with strength to stand up for myself and to recognize that even in places where I am "other" I am not a negative but a vital part of the American fabric. Attending Spelman helped me to become a woman

with more to contribute than society sometimes wants to understand. My history and my ancestry are honorable and given the opportunity and encouragement to succeed, my black sisters and I may surpass any expectation.[23]

Although there are added questions that parents and students of color should ask of the schools being considered, in other respects, the issues you face as a parent or student of color are identical to those faced by white parents and students. Assisting your son or daughter in finding a college that is right for him or her requires attention to the details, the minutiae that in the end determine whether your child has a positive, negative, or undistinguished college experience.

DISABILITY ISSUES

In spite of federal and state legislation aimed at removing barriers to people with mental as well as physical disabilities, finding a truly barrier-free school that will fully accommodate a student with disabilities is not easy. During a recent visit to a top Ivy League university, I had to trudge up two flights of narrow stairs to reach the student counseling services office. Indeed, there are not even plans in the works to redesign the building.

According to a June 22, 2000, article in the *Chronicle of Higher Education,* speakers at a presidential summit on helping disabled students make the transition to college and careers declared that the federal government and higher education officials need to do a better job of informing disabled people about how to succeed in college, and institutions should do more to help their students get jobs after graduation.[24]

The article quotes Judith E. Heumann, assistant secretary of the U.S. Department of Education's Office of Special Education and Rehabilitative Services, as saying that although more disabled students have been enrolling in college, they are not graduating at the same rate as their nondisabled peers.[25] One of the recommendations that came out of the meeting was the creation of an information clearinghouse on college admissions for disabled students.

Although matters are improving for disabled students as old campus buildings are renovated and new ones are built to comply with laws like the Americans with Disabilities Act (ADA), many campuses remain downright hostile to disabled students. Only through a visit to the campus or by reviewing a thorough audit by a disability watchdog group can parents and students determine whether a campus will be right for the student. Moreover, while litigating for compliance with the ADA is essential, the high costs of legal representation often associated with being the test case plaintiff in the litigation is generally not appealing. With more schools coming into compliance with the ADA, most parents and students may do better moving onto a campus that has already recognized the need and legal responsibility it owes to all of its students, staff, and employees.

FAITH ISSUES: CAMPUS MINISTRIES CAN BE A SOURCE OF SUPPORT

Finding a college that either supports or accepts your religious values has, on the whole, become much easier in recent years. Moreover, with some 235 Catholic colleges and universities nationally and hundreds of other firmly religiously affiliated colleges and universities of various denominations, many students never really had a problem to begin with.

Nonetheless, many students find college life quite challenging to their religious and cultural beliefs. Several years back, the case of a group of Orthodox Jewish students at Yale University, viewed by some as an aberration, underscored some of the tensions that religiously observant students may experience. The students brought a legal challenge to a Yale policy that all underclassmen live in one of the university's residential colleges. Because of their belief in modesty and that unmarried men and women should not live in close proximity to one another, the Orthodox students alleged that forcing them to live in a college dorm would violate their religious beliefs.[26]

While for most students, the college or university is able to make a religious accommodation, the students in the Yale case lost in court, but not before greatly dividing some sectors of the campus and causing the school to undertake a good deal of soul searching about its character.

So what can colleges offer to religiously affiliated students, and what advice do religious leaders have for parents and students whose religious views are being tested by college life? Today, large universities often have an interfaith coalition of chaplains committed to tolerance of one another's beliefs and collaboration on interfaith initiatives where appropriate. Harvard/Radcliffe's United Ministry, for example, bills itself as follows:

> Whether it's an issue of spirituality, an ethical question, or a personal crisis, we are here and eager to help during your sojourn at Harvard. While each of the various chaplaincies sponsors its own programming throughout the University community, there are a variety of cooperative inter-faith opportunities as well. Chaplains in the United Ministry agree to honor the religious freedom, human dignity, conscience, personal spiritual welfare, and religious tradition of every person with whom we minister.[27]

Across the country, many campuses boast a range of student religious organizations, from the Baha'i faith and various Baptist denominations to Buddhist, Catholic Fellowship, Latter-Day Saints, Newman House (Catholic), Episcopal, Friends (Quaker), Hillel (Jewish students group), Secular Humanist, Islamic Society (Muslim), Lutheran, Methodist, Unitarian, and Vedanta Society (Hindu). Parents and students interested in religious services and activities on a campus may consult Web pages or brochures created by the university that describe services available to the various religious communities on campus. Depending on the size of a religious denomination's campus presence, the group's activities may comprise informal prayer meetings, potlucks, daily religious services, active social action programs such as soup kitchens for the needy, and regularly scheduled lectures. For those who wish to mix a love of music with prayer, some campus ministries host monthly events like jazz vespers.

The uniquely American phenomenon of religious pluralism even within religious denominations may mean that a campus religious student center hosts separate religious services for several different levels of religious observance. At Harvard/Radcliffe Hillel, for example, the center hosts five worship communities and the Institute of Jewish Studies.

Aggressive proselytizing on campus is a justified concern of many parents and one against which colleges should take aggressive stands. According to the Harvard/Radcliffe United Ministry, groups that engage in these sorts of practices "have tended to be less than candid about who they are and what their agenda is, as they contact (and, in some unfortunate cases, harass) students, particularly newcomers to [the university]."[28] Parents should encourage students to contact the dean of student affairs if they feel they are being recruited or harassed by a religious cult or group known for preying on college students. Similarly, students should be encouraged to look out for their fellow students by contacting the dean's office if they feel a fellow student has become the victim of aggressive proselytizing. If your child is reluctant to report the problem or has already fallen under the spell of the cult, contact the dean of students at once and make sure to follow up so that the dean addresses the problem in a timely manner.

Maintaining their faith, questioning their beliefs, and breaking with their religious tradition are issues that commonly arise for college students of all denominations. In a conversation with Rabbi Benjamin Samuels of Newton, Massachusetts, in February 2001, Rabbi Samuels noted, "As parents we say we want to see our children gain their independence, but to some extent we also want them to be clones of us."[29] Issues that Rabbi Samuels has helped parents and students struggle with include how to maintain faith while away at college. Over the years, he has met with several students who expressed concern about observance of different ritual norms, for example, wearing a yarmulke or keeping strictly kosher, while away at school. While the students began the conversation with concerns about specific observances, over time he found that what the students were really saying is, "I'm having doubts about my general level of religious observance" or "College life is challenging my views of my religion." Clergy and parents with whom I spoke also described cases in which students have become far more rigorously observant at college than their families. This can be a source of tension as well, with children, in effect, rejecting what they view as the watered-down faith of their parents. Learning to let go in the spiritual realm may be just as important as in other aspects of your son's or daughter's life.

BALANCING WORK AND PLAY

Getting the most out of college involves working hard while keeping perspective. Student strategies for keeping stress at bay are as diverse as the student bodies at many campuses today. Dr. Anne Foster, an assistant professor of history at Saint Anselm College in New Hampshire, tends to think that, within reason, student involvement in other school activities helps rather than hurts their schoolwork:

> Usually my most-involved students are also the ones least likely to go to multiple parties each weekend, because they simply don't have time. A couple of my advisees play on the football team, and their grades are usually higher during fall semester, because their schedule is so rigidly controlled, with study time built in. Also, we know that few students, especially from a liberal arts school like Saint A's, work directly in the field they study in college. Various kinds of extracurricular activities can suggest other career paths. I have each of my students write on a card at the beginning of the semester if they have any issues (of any kind) which may affect their performance in my class. This card is how I find out about participation in team sports, school plays, learning disabilities, family problems, etc. It helps me be a little proactive when a student

begins missing class, because I can ask if it's related to that issue listed on the card.

But I also use it as an occasion to remind students that they are now in charge of managing their own time, and they need to be responsible about informing me about conflicts and possible missed classes and preparing for busy times, which may include asking for extensions. Some faculty get quite upset about late papers, etc., and they have a right to, but I see college as a time when students have to learn to take their own responsibilities for prioritizing. If Johnny prioritizes school play rehearsals over finishing a paper for me, there will be consequences, but he knows how to weigh them. Most students do pretty well. I worry more about the students who do not seem to be involved in anything.[30]

Many colleges and universities have wonderful intramural sports, music, and art programs, as well as college radio and television stations, college newspapers, and community service programs (discussed in chapter 1). Encouraging the involvement of your child in these activities may help him or her make the difficult transition from living at home to being away at school. In one or more of these activities, your child may find common ground with fellow students or make the connection to an important part of his or her former life as a high school student.

(ACADEMIC) DISTRACTIONS

The social pressures new college students face only serve to underscore the importance of students becoming genuinely engaged in their academics and building resilience through participation in extracurricular activities. Regrettably, on many campuses for too many students, play has come to mean nothing more than drinking. In their May 11, 2000, article for the *Education Law Reporter*, Christopher T. Pierson and Lelia B. Helms put it this way, "What do college students do for fun? Drink! Sixty-three percent of college students ranked drinking, including bar-hopping and partying, as their favorite activity."[31]

Given the great lengths that many campuses go to foster healthy activities for students, the focus for many on drinking suggests schools may have less control over the behavior than we tend to think. According to Dr. William DeJong of the U.S. Department of Education's Higher Education Center for Alcohol and Other Drug Prevention, in acknowledgment of the widespread perception that drinking is what college students do when they are not studying, many colleges are developing media campaigns that can be used to reinforce the true social norms among college students—a norm of moderation.[32] In research on college student social norms, Dr. DeJong and the staff of the Social Norms Marketing Research Project have found that college students grossly overestimate the percentage of their peers who engage in high-risk drinking. According to Laura Gomberg, the project's codirector based at Education Development Center, Inc.'s (EDC's) Health and Human Development Programs in Newton, Massachusetts, "This misperception can make the problem even worse by inducing students to change their own behavior toward the exaggerated 'norm.'"[33]

Creative prevention programs and the use of thoughtfully developed media messages to publicize the true drinking norms on campus at Western Washington University, the University of Arizona, and Hobart and William Smith Colleges, among other schools, appear to have turned misperceptions around. But as most health communications experts have concluded from the research, thoughtful media messages should not be fear-based. Summarizing this consensus in an interview with me in January 2001, Dr. DeJong explained, "Fear-based media campaigns are extremely difficult to execute and rarely succeed."[34]

As successful as the model prevention programs have been, parents should not expect good social norms messages alone to keep their children out of harm's way. Whatever the reasons college students tend to drink, parents can do a great deal to teach their children about all of the healthy activities they should be engaging in when they are not studying. Athletics, music groups, campus media, theater, and other campus clubs and activities are just some of the most obvious activities students can be encouraged to look to when they are not going to class or studying. Parents may want to look at their own behavior when they are not working and ask themselves what sort of behavior they have modeled for their children. Other than television, do we have leisure-time hobbies? Are we amateur musicians, gardeners, woodworkers, or joggers? Promoting your child's healthy interests may mean encouraging your daughter or son to take her or his hobby along to college. The last thing a teenager would want to do is abandon a cherished activity just when he or she is leaving for school. At this most transitional of times, teenagers should be encouraged to cling to what little stability they can find, especially when it involves healthy activities.

As for the "work hard and play hard" philosophy advocated by some, I simply do not believe it benefits anyone. Even in Holland, where fraternities and sororities are in the mainstream of student life and tend to have an academic focus, Dutch university administrators, like their American counterparts, increasingly worry about high-risk student drinking and hazing injuries. In 1999, a student at Delft University was severely injured in a fight during initiation, and in 1997, a Dutch student drank himself to death during initiation.[35]

Here in the United States, at Ivy League schools where Greek organizations are generally not a source of the problem, the work hard, play hard philosophy exerts its negative influence as well. In an interview for this book, one Harvard graduate noted, "At my college, this mentality was used to justify not sleeping. Lots of kids I knew (myself included) competed to sleep the least. My junior year roommate liked to say, 'Sleep is a waste of time.'"[36]

In any event, the Dutch argument that fraternities and sororities provide a good environment for students to study hard by day and play hard at night is no longer the case here. The *Chronicle of Higher Education* goes on to say, "Unlike Greek houses in the U.S., fraternities and sororities in the Netherlands have a tradition of encouraging academic achievement [and] the Dutch versions have a habit of sponsoring lectures and cultural outings, events that most Americans would not associate with fraternities."[37] According to Pierson and Helms' study of forty years of litigation over alcohol on campus, published in the *Education Law Reporter*, "The case law data confirm the uncomfortable relationship between colleges and fraternal organizations in terms of students' drinking."[38]

Peter Lake, a professor of law at Stetson University College of Law and coauthor of *The Rights and Responsibilities of the Modern University*, believes one of the greatest lies is the "work hard, play hard" myth that students perform well academically in spite of their regular participation in high-risk or dangerous drinking. In an interview with me in February 2001, Professor Lake said a student simply cannot party hard and then expect to perform well academically:

> I am an educator, and I know otherwise. For one thing, grade inflation and the rise of standardized testing can easily mask the lowering of certain learning functions. Common sense and experience show what is lost. Students have sometimes made a weeknight their party night. The next day in class they are less able to recall cases, to think analytically, and to pay attention. Other students—the nondrinkers or those that drink moderately—lose valuable classroom experiences while waiting for other students to function. When only a few students come to class after a night of hard partying, the class can still function; when a large number have partied too much the night before, the class begins to break down, and the entire group suffers.[39]

ROSE-COLORED GLASSES

Parents often view college life through the rose-colored glasses of their own experience. For the current generation of college parents, these views more often than not may have included personal experience with illicit drug use and heavy drinking. This view of college life tends to minimize the issues at hand. Parents need to realize that the high-risk or dangerous drinking culture of today features behavior at the margins that is quantitatively and qualitatively different from the sort of student behavior that they are recalling so fondly from their college years.

Another significant difference between the years when we went to college and today is the much greater appreciation and sensitivity that has developed identifying criminal behavior as criminal, even if it occurs on campus and between "nice kids"—upstanding middle-class college students. Perhaps the most clear-cut illustration of this shift is the widespread appreciation we have today of acquaintance rape as rape.

Students themselves often express remorse for their involvement in the riskiest forms of behavior. Recent studies, including one by researchers at the Harvard School of Public Health, show that overwhelming numbers of students favor more structure on campus and the aggressive sanctioning of violent and destructive student behavior—not less.[40] Perhaps the answer, then, for us as parents is to have more trust in the judgment of our adult children. As parents we can foster that judgment by demonstrating to them our trust and regard for their thinking.

FIVE

Bottles, Kegs, and Other Vices

◨ ◨ ◨

An entire chapter devoted to alcohol and other drugs? Is there really that much to say to cover a whole chapter? Bear with me for a bit. Take, for example, the story I was told recently by a health educator at a large, prestigious urban university on the East Coast. A student referred for counseling by the student disciplinary board had come in to meet with the health educator about his drinking problem. The student listened politely for a while, humoring the health educator as she worked her way through a litany of healthy campus activities that do not involve dangerous levels of drinking. Finally, the student could take it no longer and launched into a lecture of his own, "Yeah, but if I drink ten pints in an hour, I can get my picture up on The Wall of Fame at the Blarney Stone." This illustrates what parents and student affairs staff at many colleges are up against.

The high level of concern of both parents and college administrators with student drinking and illicit drug use is evident in the sheer volume of news articles, campus publications, and television specials devoted to the topic. In recent years, in my work at the U.S. Department of Education's Higher Education Center for Alcohol and Other Drug Prevention (www.edc.org/hec) and as a consultant to colleges, Greek organizations, and boards of higher education, I have noticed a steady flow of requests from college conference organizers for presentations about alcohol law and policy issues, prevention, campus safety, and parental concerns. The very existence of my job seems to speak to the scope of the problem and the level of administrator and parent concern over high-risk drinking and illicit drug use on college campuses.

Research and statistics on the level of college student drinking and illicit drug use abound, and some of it is quite reliable. Parents with college-bound children will also want to become familiar with the level of drinking and drug use among high school students locally, since, for many students, this is where it all starts. One caveat, however: whatever the national, state, or even local data tell you, the most important information will be your son's or daughter's personal experience with drinking and drug use.

A Few Words for Parents about Alcohol and College is a free publication produced during the late 1990s by the Michigan Department of Community Health. It cites that some 77 percent of Michigan college students have consumed alcohol within the past month—about the same level as on campuses around the country. The booklet goes on to describe why parents should care and what they should explain to their children about the impact of drinking on academic performance, professional development, and the legal environment.[1] Many other states have similar brochures for parents or are in the process of creating one.

A report released in June 2000 by the Centers for Disease Control and Prevention (CDC) found that drug use among American teenagers has significantly increased over an earlier CDC study. The CDC report was based on a confidential 1999 survey of 15,349 teenagers in grades nine through twelve in high schools throughout the United States. According to the report, half of the teens had at least one drink of alcohol, 35 percent had smoked cigarettes, 27 percent had smoked marijuana, and 4 percent had tried cocaine in the month before the survey. The study also showed that one-third of the students surveyed had consumed five or more drinks of alcohol at least once. Cocaine and marijuana use among the students surveyed was higher than in a 1993 study. The CDC researchers found that during the previous month, 33 percent of teens had ridden with a driver who had been drinking, 15 percent had used inhalants, and 9 percent had used methamphetamines.[2]

As the CDC report and other studies confirm, many students come to college with a good deal of experience with alcohol and other drug use. Equally noteworthy is that all too often, out-of-control student drinking and acts of vandalism and interpersonal violence go hand-in-hand. In a 1999 address to the National Press Club, Pennsylvania State University President Graham Spanier noted that high-risk drinking poses a real threat to both higher education and society generally:

> A companion concern to academic integrity is the challenge of developing character, conscience, citizenship, and social responsibility in our students. In my view, this is one of the most fundamental problems facing higher education today. No aspect of this challenge is greater for our young adults than the excessive consumption of alcohol and the behaviors that surround it.[3]

Like it or not, President Spanier is talking about *your* son or daughter. But parents and students need to know that eloquent and sober expressions of concern do not always translate into action and a well-articulated campus policy on high-risk and dangerous drinking.

Parents and students should also be aware that college cultures do change over time; the high school senior's image of the school may not have kept pace with the reality. Holly Sateia, the dean of student life at Dartmouth College, notes that although Dartmouth has worked long and hard to overhaul its image, the "tales of yore" of Dartmouth as a hard-drinking old boys' school handed down from generation to generation through the oral tradition still largely capture the imagination of many prospective students. Having worked previously for many years in admissions, Dean Sateia has seen first-hand how much of the good work of recruiters in stressing that Dartmouth has changed is lost on students who have a different image of the college burned into their brains.[4]

DO AS I SAY, NOT AS I DO

The unprecedented level of media coverage of the issue of out-of-control college drinking has created a rare opportunity for parents to help change the way colleges and universities view and respond to this problem. Parents need to know that what colleges and universities hold up as their alcohol and other drug policy and the reality are often not one and the same. Retired Colonel Jeffrey Levy, father of a Radford University student killed during the late 1990s in a drunk driving accident, warns that "Parents don't understand just how vague the alcohol policies at many colleges and universities really are."[5]

Alcohol policy at many colleges and universities is, at best, unevenly enforced. At many schools, for instance, policies are in place that require ID checks and trained alcohol servers at campus events at which alcohol is to be served. Many schools have created elaborate risk management programs designed to make Greek organizations aware of the best practices in party management and how to run a party safely. Such programs tend to emphasize the potential legal liability of the Greek organization and its individual members in the event someone is hurt or injured at or following an event. But how effective are these programs? Josh Slater, a fourth-year architecture student at Cornell University, recalls how when he was underage, a guard checking IDs at a campus party looked at his fake ID and told him what to do to make it look a little more authentic.[6] Just because a college has an alcohol policy does not mean the school has its high-risk drinking problem under control.

Whatever your views of drinking and underage drinking, it is imperative that you and your college-bound son or daughter know and understand the college's or university's policy with respect to public intoxication. Parents and students should seek a straight answer from the college on how the school treats students who drink too much and become a danger to themselves or others. In an interview with me in May 2000, Colonel Levy said, "Even today, when you ask many of the country's university presidents what is their school's alcohol policy, they just dance around the issue without ever stating where the school stands on problems like high-risk and dangerous drinking."[7]

To their credit, a number of colleges and universities have created newsletters for parents to keep us current on issues with which we, as parents, may be concerned. The December 1999 issue of *Penn Parents,* the University of Pennsylvania's parents newsletter, featured a front page article on Penn's Working Group on Alcohol Abuse and Stephanie Ives, the university's alcohol policy coordinator.[8] Health educators like Ives welcome the attention to the problem of student drinking in publications directed at parents because such articles help inform and enlist parents in the challenging task of helping students avoid high-risk drinking as part of their college social ritual.[9]

Dean Harry Lewis's front page article "On Alcohol in the College" in the Harvard University *Parents Newsletter* speaks candidly about the challenge of controlling a widespread practice in which many underage students illegally engage. Although many students are reluctant to discuss the impact of alcohol or drug use on their lives with their parents, Dean Lewis stresses the importance of such conversations:

> It can be both important and helpful for parents to initiate the conversation. Parents play an important role in shaping students' attitudes about drinking, and conversations between them about alcohol are never a bad idea. Students who come to [Harvard's] attention because of incidents involving alcohol rarely believe that they are not in control of their behavior, which sometimes turns out to be a matter never discussed with those who know them best.[10]

In a matter-of-fact way, Dean Lewis's article stresses that Harvard's approach is not a zero tolerance one. The standard response to a simple incident of underage drinking is a warning. Repeated violations could result in a formal disciplinary action, though there has not been a disciplinary response to a simple incident of underage drinking in the past five years. Harvard's administrative, or student disciplinary, board does sanction students for alcohol-related offenses, such as physical assaults and irresponsible hosting. The board has a good Samaritan policy and does not sanction a student who seeks medical attention (or has medical attention sought on his or her behalf), as long as the only infraction is drinking.[11]

Student drinking is not an easy matter for college administrators.

Parents who heed Dean Lewis's call for help will generally be helpful to their own children as well as to college administrators who try to stand up to alumni and board members who choose to ignore the problem.

BUILDING A COLLEGE CONSUMERS MOVEMENT

Parents can help create a social movement that challenges hard drinking schools to change their culture. Jane Frantz, a Newton, Massachusetts, schoolteacher and college parent, notes how many students from her son's high school class applied to the same twenty colleges.[12] Among the sought-after schools are many small competitive New England colleges that just have not gotten it yet when it comes to dangerous student drinking. She notes how her son shakes his head at the decisions of several of his friends who chose small, albeit academically rigorous schools, known among the students as extremely hard drinking. In these cases, the schools tend to be more physically isolated campuses or schools with unusually strong Greek programs. Frantz adds, "We're all going through this together. The parents and the kids. We're all at the same place in August before the senior year when everyone starts applying, and we're all together in April when the kids get their acceptances [and rejections]."[13]

And yet relatively few parents and college-bound students have the courage to vote with their wallets and applications against the many colleges and universities that are still saying heavy drinking is just a harmless rite of passage. Frantz notes, "Many parents just still don't know what is going on and that it *isn't* harmless."[14]

As with our concern with child care when our children are young, the issue of college student drinking is only perceived to affect us during that relatively brief window of our lives when we are involved. Once a son or daughter has been accepted to college, we seem to bow out, as if all is now well with the world. A key goal of this book is to keep open the lines of communication between parents and their children, and also between parents and college administrators, if need be, once college begins.

Why are we so stymied by the student drinking problem? Echoing the view of higher education legal scholars, Professor John Gardner of Brevard College in North Carolina explains that for the past thirty-five years American universities have been in the process of abandoning the concept of in loco parentis.[15] In an interview in the Spring 2000 issue of *Prevention File,* Dr. Gardner explained his belief that in part the widespread drinking that we see today—particularly abusive drinking—is possible because we do not expect enough of many students. Nonetheless, Dr. Gardner is generally opposed to asking students to take pledges that they will not drink when there is not a real probability they are going to live up to the pledge. It is important, in his view, that we not ask college students to do something they would not take seriously or would ignore or be dishonest about. Dr. Gardner adds that he might be more accepting of the idea of a no-drinking pledge if the university involved were a religiously affiliated institution and it was a violation of the school's religious principles to engage in that sort of behavior. Dr. Gardner and many other experts on higher education administration express concern, however, about how far we should go in a public institution in trying to dictate and control the behavior of an individual.[16]

LET'S DO THE NUMBERS . . .

According to the Center of Science in the Public Interest (CSPI), a Washington, D.C.–based nonprofit organization committed to increasing public awareness of health concerns,

- U.S. college students spend $5.5 billion annually on alcohol.
- More of the nation's undergraduates will ultimately die from alcohol-related causes than will go on to get master's and doctorate degrees combined.
- 95 percent of violent crime and 80 percent of all vandalism on

campus is alcohol-related and is implicated in 90 percent of all reported rapes.[17]

CSPI has created a powerful Web site, www.hadenough.org, for its project targeted at college students. The site includes a section entitled "In Their Own Words . . . Students' Stories on Alcohol and Campus Life." Excerpted below are several graphic descriptions by students of their negative experiences with high-risk or what has been mislabeled "binge drinking":

> It both scares and disgusts me how dependent some students at my school are on alcohol. They can't go to a social event, or even spend the night in the dorm, without drinking. At first, a majority of us drank. It's a weak rebellion, that's really about all.
>
> Some of us went broke from all of the expensive fun. Others, like myself, just got bored and found much more entertaining things to do. But some people still drink every weekend and some weeknights too. It is beginning to take control of their lives. It's sad watching them submit themselves to liquor. It's pathetic too.[18]

Linda Devine is assistant dean of student life at the University of Oregon in Eugene. Together with Dr. William DeJong, she has written "What Parents Should Say to College Freshmen about Alcohol," a brief primer for parents of college-bound students. The helpful and short publication is reproduced in part below. The entire article is available on the Higher Education Center's Web site at: www.edc.org/hec/thisweek/tw980305.html.

> Any parent who follows the news would be rightfully nervous about sending a child to college. Tragically, students die from alcohol poisoning and alcohol-related accidents every year. . . .
>
> More parents than ever before are thinking about what to say to their children when packing them off to college. Here's our advice.
>
> First, parents should set clear and realistic expectations re-

garding their child's academic performance. National studies show that students who drink a lot of alcohol get poor grades. A decline in grades may have as much to do with partying as the difficulty of the academic work. Students who know that their parents expect sound academic work will be more devoted to their studies and have less time to get in trouble with alcohol.

Second, parents should encourage their child to get involved in community volunteer work. Such work provides opportunities to develop job-related skills and to gain valuable experience. But helping others also takes young people outside of themselves, giving them a healthier perspective on the opportunities they enjoy, and it helps structure their free time.

Third, parents should encourage students to stand up for their right to a safe environment that enhances their intellectual growth. Students who themselves are not binge drinkers report being affected by the behavior of those who are, ranging from interrupted study time to physical assault and unwanted sexual advances. Students should let residence hall staff know about these problems so that action can be taken.

Fourth, parents should make sure that their child is prepared to intervene when a classmate is in trouble with alcohol. Nothing is more tragic than an unconscious student being left to die when others fail to recognize the jeopardy that student is in or fail to call for emergency help for fear of getting the student in trouble. No one wants to look back on a needless death and think "what if."

Fifth, parents should inform themselves about the alcohol scene on campus and talk to their child about it. The fact is that students themselves grossly exaggerate the alcohol and other drug use of their peers. . . . Research suggests that students who are highly influenced by their peers will "drink up" to what they believe is the norm. Confronting these misperceptions about alcohol and other drug use is key.

Advice that parents of younger children get still applies.

Parents of college students should openly and clearly express their concern about and disapproval of underage drinking and dangerous alcohol consumption. And they should present a positive role model through their own responsible use of alcohol, if they drink. Parents cannot actively monitor their children who attend college and no longer live at home, but it's just as important to be available to talk and, most important, to listen.[19]

A final word about the problems caused by college student drinking and keeping focused on those problems. According to Dr. William DeJong,

Alcoholism is not defined in terms of how much people drink, but by the impact of drinking on their lives. Likewise, we should define problem drinking on campus in terms of its attendant problems, not simply by the amount of alcohol being consumed. These problems include rape, drunk driving, violent assaults, injury, overdose, unplanned and unsafe sex, and vandalism. . . . [Smart] campus officials, parents, and students themselves are worried about safety, not the level of alcohol consumption per se.[20]

THE "OTHER DRUGS": MARIJUANA, COCAINE, LSD, SPEED, AND HEROIN

These old standbys have been around campus for so long, what can I add about them? Today's marijuana is better, or stronger, than ever thanks to the hydroponic growers and boutique breeders who have long tinkered with the varietal hybrids that contain higher THC (tetrahydrocannabinol) content. The same goes for the quality of heroin. With purity and quality up and cultivation having moved closer to home—to countries like Columbia and Mexico—a subculture of college students has discovered they can get high by smoking or snorting the drug rather than via injection. As the public at large has become more removed from the 1970s images of menacing-looking junkies with needles in their arms, a small but significant minority of students has experimented with this dangerous and illicit drug.[21]

Cocaine and speed (methamphetamine), and to a far lesser extent, crack, are all "popular" on campus too and pose serious risks to those who become involved with these dangerous drugs. According to Steve Hedrick of the California Attorney General's Office, methamphetamine is a drug with which California law enforcement is particularly concerned because of its low cost to manufacture and purchase, the damaging and lasting effects of meth labs on the environment, and the devastating health effects meth's use can have on even "casual" users.[22]

Parents should also know that LSD, psilocybin (or psychedelic mushrooms), peyote, and other hallucinogens continue to find favor among some campus subcultures. Yesterday's Dead Heads, many of whom favored, or at least experimented with, "electric" drugs like LSD (windowpane and microdot, to name two favorites) and peyote, may be today's followers of the talented though derivative acid rock bands Phish and Guster. So what is a parent to do? I for one do not favor book burning or banning my children from listening to certain music, and surely not *all* Phish or other wanna-be Grateful Dead sound-alike band fans or college students in tie-dye are poster children for psychedelic drug use. In all candor, we simply cannot keep a young person hell-bent on experimenting with psychedelic drugs from experimenting with them. Perhaps the most parents can do is be aware of their appeal to some young people and learn the warning signs of a substance abuse problem among still-young teens. As Dr. DeJong notes, building resiliency at an early age is at least part of the solution.[23] Indeed, as noted elsewhere in this chapter, college is more often than not the location to which a drug-using teen migrates rather than originates.

GHB

In recent years, gamma hydroxybuterate, or GHB, as it is more commonly known, has found a place on many college campuses as the party drug of choice. GHB has also made a name for itself among college students and the public as the so-called "date rape" drug. While the drug is illegal in the United States, it is still widely available, and students often think it is a legal substance. According to Dr. Adam Rosen, a University of New Mexico psychiatrist, GHB, which is pharmacologically classified as a steroid, also goes by the names Scoop and Liquid X and was originally popular with body builders in the early 1990s.[24]

In February 2000, President Clinton signed legislation making GHB a Schedule I controlled substance like cocaine or heroin. Under the new law, it is illegal under federal law to possess the drug, and anyone possessing, manufacturing, or distributing GHB could face up to twenty years in prison. The legislation is named after two Michigan teenagers who died after GHB was slipped into their drinks at a party.

According to college and university students on a number of campuses nationally, GHB is still readily available. Increased criminal penalties for its possession have, to date, done little to dampen the drug's popularity.[25]

Parents and students alike need to know that GHB's appeal to those bent on sexually abusing female party goers is that the drug makes the victim fall asleep. In addition to the obvious risks of falling asleep in potentially risky settings such as fraternity house parties, seizures and tremors are two of the drug's known adverse side effects.

Parents will want to warn their college-bound students of GHB's popularity and the danger it poses to unsuspecting students. Good advice is never to accept drinks from strangers or perhaps even from "friends" who present you with a container opened out of sight. GHB, taken together with alcohol, can be quite dangerous and may in rare instances result in death. Similarly, pairing GHB with other drugs can be extremely hazardous.

ECSTASY

Ecstasy, or MDMA, as it is clinically known, is a methamphetamine with hallucinogenic properties.[26] A so-called "designer drug,"

Ecstasy gained widespread popularity as a club and rave drug during the late 1980s.

The drug, which generally comes as a pill or capsule, is also known as XTC, E, Adam, X, and Eve. It works by stimulating the central nervous system and creating heightened energy and emotions. Ecstasy works by causing the release of increased levels of serotonin, a neurotransmitter that regulates the perception of appetite, mood, pain, and memory. Given the way it affects a user's emotions and stimulates feelings of euphoria, Ecstasy is thought of as a hybrid drug with some of the effects of hallucinogens such as LSD and stimulants such as methamphetamine.

The drug is said to heighten people's sense of touch and taste and to cause them to lose inhibitions. Weightlessness is another sensation commonly experienced by Ecstasy takers.

According to Dr. Rosen, the effects of Ecstasy can last for up to eight hours and may cause an increased heart rate and blood pressure and sleep deprivation.[27] As with other stimulants, side effects of the drug's use may include feelings of paranoia, dehydration, and loss of sex drive and appetite. Nonetheless, use of the drug is widespread in college and university communities, particularly in association with raves—sometimes described as large free-form dance parties featuring repetitive computer-generated music. For those who enjoy the feelings they experience when taking the drug, crashing or coming down off the drug is an okay price to pay. Perhaps fans of the drug would sober up faster reading a 1997 Johns Hopkins University study that showed that Ecstasy causes damage to the brain by reducing the number of functioning serotonin transporters.[28] Whether or not such damage is permanent is still not known, though an increased risk of kidney failure, heart attack, and stroke have been related to frequent use of the drug, which can be tolerance-building. The Drug Enforcement Agency (DEA) has classified Ecstasy as a Schedule I drug of no valid clinical use.

So-called "herbal" Ecstasy is made with ephedra, a common ingredient in diet pills. It is still legal in the United States and is also cause for parental and student concern.

KETAMINE (SPECIAL K)

Ketamine, also known as Special K, is a psychedelic anesthetic, a type of hallucinogen developed for use in veterinary surgery. Depending upon the dosage in which it is taken, ketamine's effects may mimic those of depressants, hallucinogens, anesthetics, or stimulants. Drinking alcohol or taking the drug together with a depressant can intensify its effects.

The most common symptoms of ketamine use include dilated pupils, nausea, impaired coordination, and severe mood swings. Flashbacks for weeks after use, amnesia, and paranoid or delusional thinking have also been reported.[29]

ANTIDEPRESSANTS AND OTHER PHARMACEUTICAL DRUGS

In the late 1990s reports began circulating that teens who were being treated for depression were selling or giving their medication to friends who were not themselves depressed. Given the explosive growth in recent years of the diagnosis of depression and the public's growing dependence on medication for its treatment, this phenomenon is really not that shocking. The growing acceptance of the notion of "better living through chemistry"—a phrase which oddly enough came into the American lexicon through the summer of love counterculture—is, to me, one of the most profound social developments of the end of the twentieth century. Although I welcome the public's embrace of the issue of mental health, I cringe at the widespread and seemingly unregulated public marketing of pharmaceutical medication. Be it antidepressants or antihistamines, the "talk to your doctor about . . ." billboards, magazine advertisements, and television spots with which we are inundated daily have redefined American attitudes toward medication. Whether this is for the best remains to be seen. Undoubtedly, however, it has made that much more difficult the task of explaining to our children that drugs taken without medical supervision can be extremely dangerous to your health.

With respect to all of the dangerous drugs described above, why anyone would mess with them is beyond me. Nonetheless, my heavier emphasis in this chapter on high-risk and dangerous drinking rather than on other drug use stems from the extensive research conducted in recent years that conclusively documents the far more widespread and negative impact that excessive drinking by college students has on the students themselves and on the public at large.

PARENTAL NOTIFICATION: FACT OR FICTION?

Following the fall 1998 enactment by Congress of the Amendments to the Higher Education Act, I wrote an article for *Prevention File* that received widespread distribution through the Higher Education Center for Alcohol and Other Drug Prevention's Web site (www.edc.org/hec) and through a Center reprint. The interest with which the article was greeted by both the public and the media sent a clear message: parents are desperate for information they can use to help their children make the often difficult adjustment to college and university life. In writing the article, and now this book, I do not feel that parental notification is the holy grail. I do, however, believe that staying involved in the lives of our children even after they leave for college, or turn eighteen, or even twenty-one, will benefit both our children and us as parents. The article reads, in part, as follows:

> It happens every weekend. A son or daughter, away at college for the first time, drinks him- or herself into a drunken stupor at an off-campus bar. Around 3:00 A.M. two less intoxicated friends help their roommate, hardly able to stand, onto the "Happy Bus," the local college shuttle, where they join nine other similarly inebriated undergraduates for the bumpy ride back to campus. This trip is an uneventful one. No major fights ensue and none of the dozen heavily sotted souls on this outing lose it on the way back to their dorm room. Upon staggering off the bus at the college student union, several of the more intoxicated students are approached by campus police. What is happening here? Quickly the drunk and underage

students are advised that they are being charged with violating the school's policy against underage drinking. The students are written up and told that under a newly enacted disciplinary policy their parents will be notified that the students have been charged with violating the school policy and state law.

Can a school really challenge high-risk student drinking in this manner? New education legislation aimed at college student drinking and drug use was one of several major legislative initiatives passed during the recently completed 105th Congress. At first glance, these new laws appear to represent important developments in the evolving attitude of the public towards student drinking and drug use and disorder. But some question the conviction with which the new approaches will be embraced, and the debate rages on about whether student privacy rights prohibit approaches like parental notification. Indeed, perhaps no enactment has been more widely debated than section 952, *Alcohol or Drug Possession Disclosure,* of the Higher Education Act.[30]

Signed into law in October 1998, the new law permits schools to disclose to parents violations of not only local, state, and federal laws, but also school policies and rules governing the use or possession of alcohol or controlled substances. The parental notification amendment came about largely as a result of the efforts of the father of a Virginia college student killed during the prior year in an alcohol-related accident. As enacted, the law permits but *does not require* schools to notify parents of a student's alcohol or other drug violation.

A close observer of campus alcohol policy, Jessica Kirshner, a senior at Harvard University, has the following to say:

> I have seen underage students who got drunk at campus parties sent before the disciplinary board, but I have not seen any expulsions. Typically, they get put on probation. It doesn't look good for the time being, but assuming there is no subsequent violation, the charge gets taken off the student's record by the end of the term.[31]

In Kirshner's view, in Cambridge and Boston at least, there is very little concern among students about underage drinking, and parental notification is not even a concern. She adds, "I don't know if underage drinking would be considered a rite of passage; it's just something to do." As for the types of drinking taking place among underage students, "it tends to depend on the venue. Around the dorms it's not binge drinking or heavy drinking. Heavy drinking sitting around your room is not 'socially acceptable.' But once you get out in the bars, there it is heavier."[32]

Others, however, differ with Kirshner over the willingness of college judicial boards to sanction students for alcohol policy violations. As one former member of one of those boards at Harvard sees it, board members are often too heavy handed with policy violators. "Putting aside the serious offenders, the rape and other criminal conduct, I've seen boards come down extremely hard on students who simply had one too many," notes the former board member.[33]

Before passage of the federal parental notification law, officials at most colleges and universities had refused to tell parents about student drug and alcohol violations, citing the Family Educational Rights and Privacy Act (FERPA), also known as the Buckley Amendment, a 1974 law on the privacy of student records. Nonetheless, some parents had for years argued that they have a right to be alerted to their children's life-threatening habits. Now the new law is causing many college administrators to rethink their position on parental notification, although a few schools had changed their policies even before Congress acted.

In my experience, many college administrators now think that both students and their parents need to assume more accountability and responsibility for their actions. But before the recent media focus on the problem of high-risk student drinking, most parents had little sense of the scope of the problem. Those who did know, more often than not, saw it as the aberrant behavior of someone else's son or daughter.

While campus safety advocacy groups like Security on Campus view parental notification as an important first step, they remain skeptical about the willingness of most colleges to take meaningful steps to address the heavy drinking that has become a way of life for too many college students.[34] Even at those schools that have adopted a parental notification policy, relatively few notifications will be made. At most colleges, a report will be made only if there is evidence of a severe legal or disciplinary violation. Even now, many campus police will not even consider apprehending heavily intoxicated students unless they are engaging in serious criminal behavior.

In the experience of Jeffrey Levy (Security on Campus board member), the college presidents want this problem to go away, but they do not want to be seen by students as the heavy. According to Levy,

> The sight of two sober students carrying a passed-out student into the dorm should trigger a college to say, "You are in violation of my policy." But it doesn't. I want to see more colleges stand up and say, "Binge or problem drinking is against my policy."[35]

For all intents and purposes, on most campuses there is no law against public intoxication.

Although basically, it is all up to the college or university whether or not to adopt a parental notification policy, parents and students should have input on the desirability of such a policy at the particular school. If your son or daughter is considering a school that has not considered the issue, you may want to find out what other important policy matters the college has not considered. Indeed, a college's alcohol policy generally is a good bellwether issue around which parents and students may wish to test the merchandise, so to speak.

Parental notification can really set the stage for the challenge facing parents and high school seniors making the rounds of colleges every fall. What kind of school do I want for my son or daughter? What was my college experience, and do I want my child to repeat it?

UNDERAGE DRINKING: THE REALITY VERSUS THE LAW

Although I do think parents can help build a social movement that forces colleges to confront high-risk and dangerous drinking, attempts to legislate against underage drinking are a losing proposition. College administrators can only do so much. Given the climate in which we live, no parent today should be so naïve as to think their son or daughter has not heard about drinking, witnessed it him- or herself, or done it all before. Even if this is not the case, proceeding as if your child has tasted a bit too much from the fruit of the vine is a good way to go.

Like so many other well-intentioned but poorly conceived legislative initiatives, state laws that raised the drinking age to twenty-one never had a prayer for compliance. While no sane person would quarrel with the arguments of Mothers Against Drunk Driving (MADD) that the twenty-one-year-old drinking age has contributed to a significant decline in the number of highway traffic deaths, I am convinced that the credit belongs primarily to designated driver programs and other steps to get drunks out from behind the wheel (so-called risk reduction). Efforts to criminalize underage drinking strike me as misguided and intellectually dishonest. Though few truly believe in the ability of society to control underage drinking, we cling to the notion that we are doing all we can. Why not stop pretending to enforce the drinking age and focus instead on targeting social disorder and crime directly correlated to dangerous levels of drinking by college students? The widely hailed community policing efforts underway in Boston, San Diego, and many other cities are evidence of the success of enforcement strategies that thoughtfully target the major problems, in this case, interpersonal violence, vandalism, and noise.

To get a handle on just how widespread underage drinking is, parents should perhaps ask their college-bound son or daughter for permission to shadow them at a high school party. The disconnect between what we think things are like and what is actually going on can be startling.

TAKING STEPS TO COMBAT THE PROBLEM OF HIGH-RISK DRINKING

To give parents and students a sense of the ways in which a college or university could confront the problem of high-risk student drinking, the following briefly describes policy and practical changes the University of Pennsylvania has undertaken in recent years. The risk, of course, in profiling any one campus is its good work can be undone by an unfortunate incident or critical media coverage of a problem at the school. With that caveat, here goes.

At the University of Pennsylvania, the Working Group on Alcohol Abuse has created a multidisciplinary prevention program that is making significant strides in confronting a well-entrenched problem. Involvement in and commitment to the university's comprehensive prevention initiative includes the school's health educators, faculty, house masters (faculty who reside in the residence halls), the president, the provost, campus police, the Greek advisor, and the director of the office of student conduct. Penn has a full-time alcohol policy coordinator and a demonstrated and strong commitment to addressing high-risk drinking in the West Philadelphia community. According to the university provost, Penn has also made a $300,000 to $400,000 a year commitment over several years to promoting a healthy campus environment.[36] While Penn is not and will likely never be a dry campus, the administration is committed to upholding the law and to confronting high-risk drinking and disorder.

In seeking to address a high-risk drinking problem and to build a prevention program based on a tested public health approach, administrators at Penn and a number of other colleges nationally have moved away from prevention approaches that have focused on reaching the individual student. Alcohol and other drug prevention at Penn and these other model or promising schools has evolved over the years to emphasize collaboration across and among the varied university constituencies. Students, faculty, law enforcement, peer education, Greek life, parents, and health education figure prominently in the schools' prevention initiative.

Extensive programming and materials are targeted at high-risk groups such as athletes, Greeks, and others identified through campus surveys as being at higher risk for substance abuse. Prevention messages are also emphasized in written materials sent to newly admitted students, their parents, and as part of a pre-frosh program for two hundred students that takes place the summer before the start of the freshman year. Penn is also an active member of a Philadelphia-area college prevention consortium. According to Dr. William DeJong of the Higher Education Center, consortia are important because they help colleges in close proximity to one another to pool their resources and avoid duplication of effort.[37] Moreover, colleges in the same community are often dealing with the same rogue bars (bars that will serve anyone regardless of age or level of intoxication) and other environmental factors like easy access to seemingly limitless quantities of inexpensive alcohol.

Penn is a university that has made a significant contribution to fostering students' commitment to community service. Though too early to tell whether this commitment will help reduce the incidence of high-risk drinking, as noted previously, many administrators view this change as a positive one likely to help students become involved in more than just wild partying in their free time.

The University of Pennsylvania is also moving away from the housing of students in freshman-only residence halls. Penn's thinking is that upper-class students will help informally mentor younger students and model better behavior.

As noted above, Penn is not a university that has a desire to go alcohol-free. In the late 1990s, following the death of an alumnus at an on-campus fraternity house party, a total campus ban on parties serving alcohol was mightily resisted by students and many faculty and administrators alike. The university, a large urban campus of 10,000 undergrads and 10,000 graduate students, prides itself on being the "social Ivy." Penn students consider themselves mature adults able to take responsibility for their actions. Penn's prevention program has accordingly sought to aggressively confront dangerous drinking and its related negative consequences—behaviors such as vandalism, aggravated assault, and sexual assault, as well as quality of life concerns including noise. Located in West Philadelphia, a neighborhood known as somewhat unsafe, the university has a police department that is today a highly professional organization very much committed to community or problem-oriented policing. Penn police patrols extend to Forty-third Street, several blocks beyond the Penn campus, and often target problem locations at which Penn students tend to drink and party. These locations include bars and private residences that have come to be known as popular out-of-control party locations.

Penn has a good Samaritan policy that states the university will not take disciplinary action against anyone who seeks medical attention for themselves or someone else who appears to be dangerously intoxicated. While on paper this works well, in practice many students remain reluctant to bring in a drunken classmate if they themselves have been drinking. At Penn and many other schools, students continue to go off campus to drink out of concern that their confidentiality will not be maintained. Ironically, according to Penn student affairs personnel, it is sometimes the aggressive student journalists at the *Daily Pennsylvanian*, the highly regarded campus newspaper, who violate the students' privacy. When students are admitted to the Penn hospital for drinking, they are identified by the residence hall in which they live, and in no time, everyone knows which student was involved.

Michelle Goldfarb, a lawyer and director of Penn's Office of Student Conduct, firmly believes that a so-called zero tolerance approach to alcohol policy violations or underage drinking would be a disaster at Penn.[38] Offenses referred to Penn's disciplinary board are serious offenses—not students caught with a single can of beer. Penn has also created a streamlined process for handling lesser disciplinary offenses that occur in the residence halls. This efficient system helps the university prioritize the important cases that require Office of Student Conduct review.

In a review I conducted in 2000 of Penn's prevention program, I was particularly impressed with the Penn police department's approach to problem off-campus residences and vendors. In response to a question about how they confront such locations, Thomas King, deputy chief of investigations with the university's police department, detailed a strategy in line with the problem-oriented or community policing approach.[39] Deputy Chief King described how the department gets officers out to the locations in advance of big party weekends to gently (or not so gently) warn persons of the law, local health and safety codes, and the licensing and enforcement authority of the Pennsylvania Liquor Control Board (PLCB). The Penn police have less reach and authority with locations in the Center City District of Philadelphia and other areas farther from the campus.

While the Penn approach may not be right for all colleges and universities, the university's program is thoughtfully developed and quite comprehensive, firmly rooted in the Higher Education Center's prevention approach (the national model of college alcohol and other drug prevention). Penn recognizes the importance of confronting the various factors that contribute to an environment that fosters out-of-control college student drinking. Alcohol and drug awareness programming for freshmen, Greeks, athletes, and other high-risk groups; parental involvement; new student mailings; well-prepared orientation materials; community service; student activities and athletics; treatment for those in need; faculty mentoring; new living arrangements; and an aggressive social norms marketing campaign (aimed at correcting student misperceptions about the extent of drinking that goes on at Penn) are all the sorts of things colleges need to be doing to address this problem. Involvement in a strong multi-university campus prevention coalition, sensible enforcement and student disciplinary procedures, and an emphasis on personal responsibility are other important aspects of Penn's program.

HARD QUESTIONS FOR ADMINISTRATORS ABOUT ALCOHOL AND OTHER DRUGS

In the preceding pages, I have cited several informative brochures that parents and their college-bound sons or daughters may wish to read before leaving for the college tour. Another short article for all parents or future college parents is "What College Catalogs Don't Tell You about Alcohol and Other Drugs on Campus" by William DeJong and Karen Zweig of the U.S. Department of Education's Higher Education Center. The article, which is unfortunately no longer available, was published by the Higher Education Center, and is excerpted as follows:

> Most college-bound students and their parents want to find a college where students can learn and also have fun, a place where students won't feel pressured to drink or take drugs, and where they won't have to deal with problems created by classmates who misuse alcohol and drugs.
>
> Here are some steps you can take to make sure the college you select will provide a safe, healthy environment that will foster the academic and social development of all students.
>
> *Ask the Admissions Office for Copies of These Documents*
> * School newspapers. What alcohol or drug-related messages are expressed in the ads, articles, editorials, or letters to the editor?
> * The college's or university's policies regarding alcohol and other drug use.
> * The biennial review the college is required to undertake under the Drug-Free Schools and Communities Act. This review should report on the effectiveness of the school's alcohol and other drug prevention program and the consistency with which the school's policies are enforced.[40]

DeJong advises that by comparing copies of these documents from several different schools, parents will be able to get a sense of how committed each one is to addressing drinking and drug use issues.[41] Do not be fooled by silence or brevity—that does not necessarily mean there are not significant problems at the school. A more detailed report, more extensive policies, or more attention to these issues in the campus newspaper often indicates that a school is taking crucial steps to address the problems that do exist, rather than ignoring them.

Following are more suggestions from DeJong and Zweig:

Questions Parents Can Ask the Admissions Officer

By telephone, letter, or in person, you can learn a great deal by asking questions such as these:

- Has the president appointed a committee or task force to draft, review, and revise the school's policies to reduce or avoid alcohol and other drug problems? If yes, what are they doing?
- What is the college's policy regarding alcohol advertising or other marketing activities on campus?
- What changes has the college made in its curriculum or academic calendar to reduce student misuse of alcohol and other drugs? For example, what has been done to prevent "weekends" from starting on Thursday night?
- What options are available to students during spring break?
- Has the college established substance-free housing for any students, including freshmen, wishing to live in an environment that is completely free of alcohol and other drugs?
- Has the college joined with local community leaders, law enforcement personnel, and businesses to curtail illegal underage access to alcohol?
- Is alcohol sold on campus? Why or why not? Where, when, and to whom?

A form letter for requesting this information from a school is available from the Higher Education Center's Web site: www.edc.org/hec.

What to Look for When You Visit a Campus

- Check the bulletin boards and campus newspapers. Do you find ads from bars or liquor stores? Do notices for events seem to promote alcohol consumption, or do they indicate that nonalcoholic drinks and food will be served?
- Wander through the residence halls. Do you see alcohol-related posters on the walls? Do students decorate their

rooms with pyramids of beer cans? Are trash cans filled with beer cans or bottles after a weekend night?

- Talk to students. Ask them what the social scene is like on campus. How easy is it for students to get drugs or alcohol? Do most students feel they need to drink to fit in or have a good time? What would a nondrinking student do to have fun on campus? How strictly and consistently are campus alcohol and drug policies enforced?
- Talk to a campus police officer. Ask how often police get called to deal with an incident where drinking or taking drugs caused a problem. How serious do they think such problems are on campus? Do they feel the campus president and deans are aware of the problems and involved in trying to solve them?
- Talk to faculty. How much of a problem do they think is posed by students who drink or take drugs? Do they see class attendance falling off as the weekend approaches?
- Walk through the commercial neighborhoods that students frequent. Are there a lot of places where alcohol is available? Do they seem to target students with their advertising? Do they offer "specials" that encourage drinking?
- During the evening, stop by student-oriented drinking environments, both on and off campus. Do servers check for IDs and appear to monitor the drinking rates of patrons? Are food and nonalcoholic beverages readily available?[42]

PROBLEMS RELATED TO ALCOHOL OR OTHER DRUG USE ON COLLEGE CAMPUSES

Students who drink or use drugs may have these problems:

- missed classes
- poor academic performance
- trouble with authorities, including arrests
- injuries
- fights or arguments
- unplanned sexual activity, possibly leading to pregnancy or sexually transmitted disease
- perpetrating acquaintance rape

Students who do NOT drink or use drugs may experience the following problems because of the behavior of other students who do:

- interrupted study or sleep
- destruction of property
- physical assault
- unwanted sexual advances
- acquaintance rape
- having to take care of a drunken or high student[43]

SIX

Health Is Academic

◘ ◘ ◘

As parents, we often do not realize just how much we do for our teenage children. If a child is college-bound, the planning for separation should begin at least two years before the student's first day of college classes. A now legendary story in my family involves a precocious cousin who went off to Cornell University at age sixteen. A few weeks into the school year, he called home and told his mother, "I brought my clothes to the Laundromat last week, and I went back today and they were gone." The story has surely been embellished over the years—to further humiliate my cousin, no doubt. Many parents, and first-year college students, will still smile knowingly upon hearing it.

So what does this anecdote have to do with health issues? Financial support aside, health is perhaps the most important area in which parents do a great deal for their grown children. Sleep deprivation, stress, depression, physical health, and, sadly, personal hygiene are some of the issues parents may find they must remind their teenage children about, even after they have left for college. Jane Frantz, a Newton, Massachusetts, high school teacher and mother of three teenagers, describes how she and her husband began weaning their eldest college-bound son off of their indulgence when he was a high school sophomore:

> We do so much for them that they don't even realize. My son has medical issues. Recognizing the need for him to look after himself, two years ago we started having him make all of his

own doctor's appointments and pick up his medication at the pharmacy. He still forgets from time to time, but at least he will be ready when he starts college in the fall.[1]

Nonetheless, when they take their son off to William and Mary in September, Jane and Richard Frantz, like many college parents, will be going along with him to visit the doctor and thoroughly review his medical concerns. They still find themselves doing other things for their eighteen-year-old that he should be doing for himself by now, like the laundry.

STDS AND OTHER INFECTIOUS DISEASES

Though one might think otherwise from all the media focus on drinking and drug use by college students, these are not the only issues of concern to parents and students. In recent years, mononucleosis, sexually transmitted diseases (STDs), yeast infections, meningitis, and other health problems have emerged as important college student health concerns. A few years back, when a friend was getting married, she met with the caterer together with her mother and fiancé. When they got to discussing flower arrangements for the tables, my friend's mother asked, "What about chlamydia?" Of course what she meant to say was clematis, a flower popular for centerpieces. Without missing a beat, the caterer replied, "Nah, you don't want that."

What about chlamydia and other infectious diseases? Although we tend not to think of college students as "at-risk," they are indeed at higher risk for a variety of infectious diseases because of the behaviors in which they tend to engage. Chlamydia and other sexually transmitted diseases are a dangerous health problem for college students, according to a physician at the after-hours clinic at a large Boston area university.[2] According to the U.S. Centers for Disease Control and Prevention, chlamydia is a sexually transmitted disease, which if left untreated in women can cause severe reproductive and other health problems including pelvic inflammatory disease (PID).

PID has been linked to infertility and potentially fatal tubal pregnancy. Chlamydia may also result in problems following pregnancy, including neonatal conjunctivitis and pneumonia. According to the CDC, untreated chlamydia in men typically causes urethral infections but may also result in other medical complications.

Regrettably, changing at-risk sexual behaviors through media and education is difficult and expensive. According to Dan Wohlfeiler, former education director of STOP AIDS and University of California–San Fransciso researcher,

> Each year fifteen million Americans get infected with sexually transmitted diseases, and college students are particularly at risk. Moreover, risky sexual behavior tends to increase as the level of alcohol consumption increases. Colleges will really need to do something to address the out-of-control drinking if they want to put a dent in the problem of STDs among college students.[3]

Echoing Wohlfeiler, public health social marketing expert Julia E. Rosenbaum of the Academy for Educational Development in Washington, D.C., explains, "'Just Say No' can't hold a candle to 'Just Do It,' particularly where young college students [men] and sex are concerned." She adds that young adults feel the pressure all around them. The important thing for parents to keep in mind is that they can play a role in reducing risk-taking. Studies have shown that teens who have talked with their parents take fewer risks, particularly fewer sexual risks. The talks do not need to be full of information, threats, or even advice. According to Rosenbaum, "Talks to show you care, you are there, and that you're interested—in who they hang out with and what they are doing—make all the difference."[4]

Other major college health service and student concerns include mononucleosis and meningitis. According to an article in the May 1998 *Daily Northwestern,*

> Colleges are a natural breeding ground for the bacteria that causes meningitis, a potentially fatal illness. During the spring of 1998 an increase in the incidence of meningococcal

meningitis prompted many colleges, including Northwestern, to heighten students' awareness of the disease.[5]

In a June 2000 report, the CDC recommended that college freshmen should be better informed about the possibility of contracting meningitis. According to the CDC committee that studied the issue, a vaccine should be available upon request at college health facilities, though mandatory vaccination was not advised. The report cited the "modestly increased risk" that the disease poses to college students, particularly first-year students housed in dormitories.[6]

According to Eric Rubin, M.D., Ph.D., an infectious disease specialist at the Harvard School of Public Health, the bacteria that cause meningococcal meningitis first live in the throat before they invade into the blood and spread to the brain.[7] Therefore, they are not spread by breathing. The bacteria are, however, spread by forms of close contact such as kissing. While in many cases the mode of transmission is unclear, the fact that the disease is transmitted among members of the same household or institution suggests that close contact can result in transmission. According to Dr. Rubin, the rate of meningitis among college students living in residence halls—4.6 per 100,000—is higher than any other age group over two years old.[8] Still, these numbers fall far short of the threshold of 10 per 100,000 required for the agency to recommend a mandatory vaccination campaign.

Annually, about one hundred college students contract meningitis, with six to eight cases resulting in death. But given the high cost of providing the meningitis vaccine to all college freshmen (and, no doubt, resistance from already overworked college health professionals), the CDC determined that it would not be cost effective to require the vaccination of students. In 1997 the American College Health Association issued a statement recommending that "colleges and universities ensure all students have access to a vaccination program for those who want to be vaccinated."[9]

Dr. Rubin describes meningococcal meningitis—the type of meningitis that concerned the CDC—as a "potentially fatal bacterial infection in the fluid of the brain and spine." According to Dr. Rubin, the closed environment of college campuses is an almost ideal medium for the bacteria that cause meningitis. Meningitis bacteria are present, though dormant, in much of the population. According to Dr. Rubin, if detected early enough, the disease may be treated with antibiotics. However, the infection spreads rapidly, and the chances of a cure decrease the longer an infected person goes untreated. Otherwise healthy persons can die from the disease in a matter of hours.[10]

Students may want to reduce the risk of contracting the rare disease by getting vaccinated. Once your son or daughter has been vaccinated, you can turn your attention to the other serious and much more common health concerns students tend to face at college.

THE FRESHMAN FIFTEEN

Though arguably not strictly a college student health concern, the common rapid weight gain by first-year college students—the so-called freshman ten or fifteen—is a legitimate parental and student health concern. To find the culprit, just visit most college campus dining halls and eating spots in the neighboring area. Indeed, with an increasing number of colleges contracting out their food service to junk/fast-food chains, this concern can be expected to grow. At many schools, the most popular student dining choices already include Pizza Hut or Taco Bell. This is probably not cooking like Mom and Dad used to do and surely is not benefiting anyone's waistline.

As quick as I am to blame the abdication of college dining services to the albeit efficient fast-food industry, the cause for the problem is actually considerably more complex. In response to criticism from students, parents, and administrators in recent years, many campuses have undertaken significant changes in their dining services to give students greater variety and healthier alternatives. Additionally, students are as much to blame for their eating habits as the fast-food outlets and plain old college cafeterias that cater to them. If there was no market for junk food, there would not be any junk food sold. That said, it does not help any when schools like Emory University in

Atlanta take money from "the real thing" in exchange for naming part of their brand-new student center the Coca-Cola Commons. According to one Emory student, "Emory is Coke U."[11]

The point is, parents and students need to be wise to just how unhealthy much of the food students subsist on really is. In a candid Student.Com article by student journalist Michelle Navarro of the *UCLA Daily Bruin*, the author writes the following:

> Walk into any dining hall and the proof is spread out before you: slices of pepperoni pizza oozing with extra cheese, plates of golden-brown Tater Tots, plump chili-cheese dogs, chocolate chip cookies, and some big brownies topped with ice cream for dessert. . . .
>
> With so many tasty choices before them in the all-you-can-eat cafeterias, many students find themselves choosing their meals based on what they can fit on their trays.[12]

Like kids in a candy store, college students, especially freshmen, tend to look at the choices and select one of each. Taking smaller portions and choosing one dessert instead of several would help. Teach your son or daughter to better monitor his or her food intake before leaving for college or simply to lay off the buffet. Remembering the motto "A moment on the lips, forever on the hips" helps somewhat as well.

According to Albuquerque, New Mexico, psychiatrist Adam Rosen, M.D., loneliness, depression, and anxiety over being away from home and family for the first time contribute to some students' tendency to overeat.[13] Students may also turn to eating when they should instead be studying, notes Dr. Rosen. He adds, "It's the perfect way to procrastinate when there's work to be done." Making a workout or sports a part of the routine is how many students fight the "spare tire" syndrome. Laying off the ubiquitous beer and salty food at college parties is another way to cut down on calories. The main point for parents and students is, no one is going to regulate the student's diet except the student once he or she leaves for college.

EATING DISORDERS

For students (and parents), eating disorders such as anorexia nervosa and bulimia present far more difficult problems than the freshman fifteen weight gain. Students who exhibit signs of such disorders either before or during college should receive professional help from a physician or mental health professional who specializes in eating disorders.

DEPRESSION AND STRESS

In his research on depression and stress, Harvard Medical School professor Dr. Ronald C. Kessler has found that an estimated 37 percent of Americans ages fifteen to twenty-four—many of whom are college students—suffer from a diagnosable mental illness.[14] Dr. Kessler, whose research is cited in a June 2000 opinion piece in the *Chronicle of Higher Education,* further notes that these forms of mental illness range "from mild and short-lived to chronic and severe . . . illnesses—including depression, anxiety, schizophrenia, and bipolar disorder—[which] can be treated."[15]

Summer M. Berman, Shari Strauss, and Natasha Verhage of the Ann Arbor, Michigan, mental health advocacy program Mentality, argue in the *Chronicle* opinion piece that "colleges and universities often act as if their students do not suffer from mental illnesses, or as if students with mental illnesses cannot function in higher education."[16] As a result, campus mental health advocates argue, few institutions provide adequate mental health services, and the support that is available is often not well coordinated.

Meg Muckenhoupt, a mental health professional and Boston-area writer, finds that many students diagnosed with a mental illness end up leaving college before completing their degrees. She notes that many of these students might have remained in school if they had only received proper treatment or counseling.[17] Given proper treatment, most mental health issues facing college students are not completely debilitating.

So what can parents do to help a son or daughter who may be prone to depression or suffer from other mental health concerns? Sylvia Epstein, Ph.D., a psychologist specializing in evaluation and assessment in Scarsdale, New York, recommends that parents who are aware that their son or daughter suffers from or is prone to depression speak with the student about their concerns and help set up therapy or help before the student starts school.[18] The reality is, as close as they may be to your child, for a variety of reasons faculty, residence hall staff, and even roommates may not be in a position to help a depressed student get help.

Mild or severe psychological problems can interfere with a student's ability to perform academically. At both Cornell University and Saint Anselm College, history professor Anne Foster has worked with a number of students struggling with psychological issues ranging from depression over a parents' divorce to anxiety from an unspecified family problem. Dr. Foster has also had students with the full range of learning disabilities, including one student who became mentally disabled following a severe car accident.

Professor Foster recommends that parents encourage their children to tell someone on campus a reasonably full version of their psychological or relevant personal history. Informing someone of an issue of concern helps make that person a discreet advocate when necessary. In Dr. Foster's experience, most faculty will be happy to accommodate requests for special consideration if these requests come early in the semester and show how the student plans to accomplish the required course work. Many faculty may be willing to accommodate the student even if it involves evaluating the student on a different schedule or on assignments that are different from those followed by the rest of the class.

The worst thing a struggling student can do is try to tough it out. If a student has a severe psychological problem, toughing it out will not work, and even the most sympathetic professor will feel manipulated if requests for special accommodation come when a student has already performed poorly. In addition, some faculty will not agree to special accommodations (and they have the right to refuse, in many cases), and it will be best if the student learns that during the add/drop period. I'd like to reiterate, though, that students should not feel compelled to "spill all" to every professor. So long as one person of some authority on campus can convey to others that the problem is real and serious, then most professors would prefer that a student maintain confidentiality. I find that lack of specific knowledge means that professors can treat the student as normally as possible, which is usually the best way to encourage him or her to function as a regular student.

In their opinion piece in the *Chronicle of Higher Education*, Berman, Strauss, and Verhage note that "professors may be the first to observe changes in a student's well-being, because of their regular contact with students. They should know how to spot possible problems, and be able to direct students to appropriate help."[19]

While I share the view that faculty should know how to spot depression and act on it, for the foreseeable future the hope that faculty and administrators will take affirmative steps to help, or put in place mechanisms for recognizing depression among students, may be little more than a pipe dream. According to Meg Muckenhoupt, "Regrettably, many colleges and universities are still years away from putting in place better systems for identifying students in need of mental health services." Muckenhoupt adds that an additional complication is that the years from eighteen to twenty-four are the age of onset for many major mental disorders.[20]

The *Chronicle* opinion piece offers several additionally important observations about the college response to student mental health concerns. In particular, the authors note how admitting to having a mental problem is often seen as admitting defeat.[21] Mental health advocates warn that seeking outside help is still often seen as admitting a weakness in one's character. College students are said to be particularly likely to hold such views as they are under great pressure to define themselves academically and socially and to meet their own high expectations, as well as those of their professors, parents, and peers.

Parents need to be aware that, in the words of Berman, Strauss, and Verhage, "Colleges and universities do not seem to want to talk about mental illness."[22] Though colleges often bury incoming freshmen with health service and counseling information, mental health service descriptions may be lacking in the brochures. Others argue that if you are depressed it is better to be in college than not in college. Nonetheless, there is considerable support for the views of Berman, Strauss, and Verhage, who say the following:

> Students with mental illnesses typically do not see themselves as disabled, and therefore do not seek out assistance from the disabilities office. Yet professors are seldom willing to make accommodations for students—like giving them extra time for exams—unless they are registered with the disabilities office.[23]

Practically speaking, parents should become familiar with some of the mental health concerns college students and college parents commonly experience. Barbara Rosen, Ph.D., a La Jolla, California, psychologist, identifies the following psychological issues college students and their parents tend to face in a son's or daughter's leaving home and heading off to school:

- depression
- separation anxiety for both parents and students
- the empty nest syndrome for the parents
- guilt and anxiety issues related to siblings left at home[24]

These issues are explored in greater detail below.

COLLEGE STUDENTS AND ANTIDEPRESSANT MEDICATION

Given the tendency of some health providers, under pressure from insurers, to cut corners, I have a good deal of reluctance about the public's growing fondness for pharmaceutical antidepressants. Moreover, as a June 8, 2000, article in the *Boston Globe* suggests, there is growing public concern that Eli Lilly and Company and other pharmaceutical companies may have been less than forthright in revealing potentially dangerous side effects in seeking patents for their medications. According to the *Globe* article as well as a stream of new books on the industry, since its creation, over "35 million people worldwide have taken Prozac, and Lilly derived more than 25 percent of its $10 billion in revenues [in 1999] from the drug."

While the jury is still out on these allegations against Eli Lilly, college students (and their parents) should seek a second opinion when a physician recommends a pharmaceutical antidepressant for their depression. Dr. Adam Rosen, the Albuquerque, New Mexico, psychiatrist, warns that the focus of college health services on medication, even without the allegations of fraud, may be misplaced.[25] Noting the popularity of Prozac for the treatment of depression, Dr. Rosen urges health service staff to carefully consider the causes of a student's depression before assuming that Prozac is the way to fix it:

> For the treatment of milder depression caused by external factors such as stress or a specific crisis, therapy may be preferable to medication. Students suffering from a chemical imbalance or with a genetic predisposition toward depression are better candidates for medication.[26]

Other mental health professionals note the commonly glossed-over relationship between antidepressants and sexual dysfunction. For a sexually active college student, these side effects can be extremely damaging emotionally.

Parents or students concerned about depression or other mental health concerns should consider consulting a mental health professional before the student leaves for college. He or she should be able to allay your concerns and/or help arrange for suitable treatment for the student while away at college. If properly treated, depression need not seriously disrupt a student's pursuit of a college degree. The point is to properly diagnose potential problems before they spiral into something more severe.

SEPARATION (ANXIETY)

For many students, particularly those who go to college close to their home, separation from family may not be as pronounced as it may be for others.

At many colleges, students tend to go home on the weekends, as do the students Professor Anne Foster has taught at Saint Anselm College and the State University of New York at Cortland. Not every student every weekend, of course, but many students go home at least one weekend per month. One view is that this situation is both self-selecting and self-reinforcing. Saint Anselm College in New Hampshire, for instance, is well-known as a regional liberal arts college, drawing many of its students from a radius of about one hundred miles. These students, many of whom could have attended college farther away from home, looked for a school within a two- to three-hour drive from their homes so that they could go home on the weekends. On the other hand, a student who chose to go to more of a "national" college close to his or her home, might stop going home on the weekends because few of his or her classmates do (or can, since they are from places farther away). Students from regional colleges with large numbers of students from homes nearby tend not to experience such a strong pull to stay at college on the weekend, since the bulk of the students can easily go home.

In Dr. Foster's view, going home too often can also be a problem, and is likely to affect college freshmen at regional colleges the most. Some freshmen lack both the focus and study habits necessary to study at home in the way they need to study. This is particularly a problem when a student is the first in her or his family to go to college or when many of the student's friends have not gone off to college. According to Dr. Foster, "What happens then is the student finds that there is no one at home who understands that studying in college is a whole different ball game than studying was in high school." She is also certain that going home too frequently can also mean a delay in a student's making friends and developing a social life at school.

Dr. Foster warns against parents and their children attempting to set any guidelines about how many visits is too many. Instead she urges parents to think about how their child is making the transition to college and encourages them to ask specific questions about assignments over the course of the semester, not just, "Do you have homework this weekend?"[27]

FAMILY PRESSURES

Not all of the health and psychological issues college students face are related to issues they are confronted with *at* college. Divorce, marital strife, and the health concerns of those remaining at home may weigh heavily on college-bound students as well. According to Andrew E. Kuhn, Ph.D., a psychologist in Katonah, New York,

> Sometimes college-bound students find themselves in the unenviable position of being a security blanket of sorts for a parent whose spouse has just left them or who is him- or herself suffering from severe separation anxiety. Though not always easy to do, some parents should be more respectful of their child's maturation and separation. Leaving home to attend college is a common and healthy ritual that parents should generally embrace rather than hinder for their personal reasons.[28]

In such instances, Dr. Kuhn advises parents going through a difficult period in their own lives to seek appropriate counseling. Letting go for a parent may mean looking elsewhere for the support the parent had hoped to find in a child. Or it may mean maintaining the bond, but via e-mail, the phone, and frequent visits, rather than nightly over dessert. Assuming you can, you may also want to talk with your son or daughter about what you are going through and why it will be hard when he or she leaves.

Coping with family health problems is a complex issue worthy of another shelf full of books. Whether or not it is borne out by the research, it seems as though more Americans are becoming ill with cancer and other diseases earlier and earlier. This means that a growing number of students will be leaving for college at a time when a mother or father is severely ill. In my limited experience, only candor between parents and a son or daughter about the illness can help the family work through issues related to the child's leaving home at this time. Inevitably, most children who leave for college at a time when a parent is ill to some extent experience feelings of guilt over having left. Moreover, for some students with a terminally ill parent or sibling, the best choice may be to defer starting or returning to school. Talking through the difficult issues is essential for parents and students. If conversations of this sort do not come naturally, parents may want to seek help from a friend who has been through a similar experience, a family counselor, or their clergy. The third party need not be a third wheel and often can help parents and children explore fears, concerns, and feelings of guilt associated with difficult life choices like leaving home at a time when a loved one is ill.

UNLOADING: SOMETIMES THEY JUST NEED TO TALK

As a parent of three grown children with six degrees between them, my father vividly recalls the dozens of late night phone calls from one or another of us away at college facing a difficult exam or having just been dumped by a girl- or boyfriend. Only now that he is a grandfather does he recognize what many of those calls were really about. "Unloading," he calls it. Once we had made the call and spilled out our hearts and fears, we almost always seemed immediately better able to cope with the situation at hand. Looking back, on most occasions my father recalls sensing that nothing he said actually helped; it was simply the act of being on the other end of the phone, ready to receive. This, of course, did not leave Mom and Pop feeling any better once we had hung up. Indeed, unaware at the time of the common pattern, they often lost sleep staying up worrying about their children's problems with exams or social adjustment. Pop's advice today: take the inevitable calls more in stride. They are indeed part of the ritual of daughters and sons away from home calling their parents to vent.

My personal favorite is not a call one of us made from college but a call one of my sisters made one summer while she was still in high school. At sixteen, she had headed off for the summer on an American Youth Hostel (AYH) bike trip through New England. Although the trips were generally supervised, going up a mountain in the rain my sister had somehow fallen behind and gotten separated from her group. The phone rings in my parents' house, and it is my sister calling to say she had gotten separated from her group.

My mother (patiently): Where are you calling from? Are you okay?

My sister: A bar. Yes, I'm fine.

My mother: How did you get there?

My sister: Some guys in a truck picked me up, and we drove here.

My mother (quite nervous): Where are you? What is the name of the bar? I'll call AYH and tell them where you are.

My sister (annoyed): It's okay. I've gotta go now. I'll call you next week. Bye.[29]

Even in that pre-cell-phone, pre-caller-ID age, my sister survived unscathed. Eventually, the tour leader located my sister. She soon made friends with the strongest kid on the trip, and he ended up carrying her saddlebags, as well as his own, the rest of the summer.

As parents we are all survivors of our own stories of this sort. Building independence and resiliency in our children means letting go in various ways. For me and my siblings, growing up meant heading off on loosely supervised bike trips, as well as unsupervised trips to Europe and across the United States. As teenagers we ran on a long leash, generally suitable for our ability to make our way alone and for the times. As parents we come from many parts of the country and the world, and our children fall into many categories. Fostering independence and responsibility well before the first day of freshman orientation arrives will surely help your child make the adjustment to college life.

KEEPING OPEN THE CONVERSATION

A child's leaving home for college is unquestionably a watershed event in the lives of both the student and the parent. According to Jonathan Benjamin, M.D., a Newton, Massachusetts, pediatrician, the toughest issue for many parents whose children are leaving for college is the separation. In his practice, Dr. Benjamin often speaks with parents concerned about their child's departure and struggling with how to help their child make the transition to college life without wanting to intrude. He gives the following advice:

> As parents, we worry about our children. While supporting their emancipation by not calling daily, we want to know how they are doing at school socially, emotionally, and academically. Many colleges seem to take too hands-off an approach, telling parents, "Well, get over it. He or she's gone now. He or she will be okay."[30]

Dr. Benjamin and other health professionals warn that many schools appear to want to have little to do with the parents once the college bill has been paid. Some universities even go as far as to delicately say, do not expect to hear from us if there are problems with your child. By hiding behind the federal Family Educational Rights and Privacy Act (FERPA), many schools tell parents that they are barred by law from reporting to a parent or guardian that a student may be having problems. That this is complete nonsense and an inaccurate reading of the law has yet to filter down to some student affairs and academic administrators.

While FERPA does govern the confidentiality of a student's "educational" records, nothing in the law bars a school from contacting a parent when a child is experiencing emotional difficulty, depression, or other problems that are interfering with his or her life at college. Indeed, this reluctance of schools to assure parents that they will be contacted if there is a problem affecting the child is owed largely to a wrongheaded legal perspective on student privacy and parental rights. Regrettably, legal counsel at many schools have read the statutory and case law to say to schools, "Do not get involved. Non-feasance is better than malfeasance." In other words, college and university legal counsel have advised administrators to instruct their staff not to promise anything to parents. If you tell parents you are going to contact them in the event of a problem and you fail to do so, then a lawsuit will be your reward.

While this may help explain the reluctance of schools to get involved, parents should not accept that this is the way things need to be. Recent changes in the case law and, more importantly, changes in the attitude of college and university legal counsel are reshaping the way schools respond to parental requests that they be contacted if their son or daughter appears to be struggling in some way. The legal issues facing parents, students, and colleges are explored in greater detail in chapter 8.

For many parents the thought of speaking with their children about social concerns is anathema. We fear rejection of our overtures, having been so often rebuffed while attempting the same during the high school years. First, parents need to keep in mind that college *is* different. The summer before a son or daughter leaves for school can be a particularly difficult period for both parents and children. Many college-bound students may feel the need to start cutting their ties with parents in anticipation of college. Some of those who are college-bound may spend the summer before leaving for college testing the limits of their relationship with parents. Common expressions of this may sound familiar, "I'll stay out as late as I want." "Get used to it. I'll be at college in a few months, and you won't have any control over what I do and when, or if, I come home." As trying as parents may find this sort of testing, it is just a son or daughter expressing fear about life once there are no rules about how late he or she can stay out.

Kit Williams, the former associate director of residential life at Boston University, advises parents to listen carefully for signs of depression or undue stress in their first-year college student. This is especially true during the first semester but really applies to the student's entire time away at college. During her many years in residential life, Williams found that depression often hit new students in the fall around mid-October—midterm time—when the work really starts heating up and demands on students are pretty high. Another difficult time for students is when it has been a long time since they had a day off. The Columbus Day weekend can be just the release some students need. Also, according to Williams, the times students tend to go home—for Thanksgiving and winter recess—always seemed to arrive just in time.[31] Thanksgiving and winter break are hard times for new students generally, since by that point they have been away at school for a few months and have likely felt as if they have changed from their high school persona. By the time the holidays arrive, many students are struggling with questions such as:

- Will my family notice how I have changed?
- How will I fit back in with the family?
- How will my relationships with friends from home have changed?

Williams's final advice to parents is to make a personal connection with residence life staff when dropping off a son or daughter at college:

> I think parents should try to meet the RA and hall director or the equivalent when they drop their child off. It gives them a sense of who is in charge and who to call if there is something going well or poorly. It also gives them a familiar contact to at least start with if they see issues they need addressed.[32]

WHERE TO TURN IF YOUR CHILD HAS A PROBLEM

While many colleges are doing more to keep parents apprised of college life issues and to address parental concerns about topics like drugs and alcohol and campus safety, brochures and concern are not enough. Suppose your son or daughter becomes depressed during his or her first year away at college. What happens then? Will he or she be able to find his or her way to counseling services? Will a room-mate or friend encourage your child to seek help—perhaps walk them to the counseling center? How about a resident hall advisor or a professor or coach? Most likely not. While many schools have put in place well-organized counseling service programs, whether and how students get to those services is another matter. Some will surely recognize that they need help and seek it out, but what about the others—the shy, reserved student, the student who has already developed a serious problem with alcohol or drugs, or the student immobilized by depression linked to loneliness, academic or social stress, or mental illness? For all too many college students, there simply is no mechanism for connecting with the much-needed services. While most students are literally surrounded day and night by people who could help, only a few generally step forward and take the initiative to confront a depressed or drug-abusing student. Why?

Let us start with the largest group of bystanders—college students. The fact is, these individuals are, by and large, not trained to recognize the signs of a problem. They are not professionals trained in mental health issues or substance abuse treatment. A course or two may help, but that is often as far as it goes. As for residence hall staff, their training and exposure may be almost as limited. And as for faculty, deans, and other administrators, they often do not see intervening as part of their job, or worse, not in the best interest of the university.

Discussing this reality, Dr. Benjamin, a Massachusetts pediatrician, says, "Many kids who develop problems simply get lost. I think too many schools have fallen down on the job in not creating a structure for students who don't know how or lack the capacity to access services."[33]

Dr. Benjamin and other physicians believe that colleges and universities need to be much more proactive in looking after undergraduates:

> Let's face it, most first-year college students are *not* independent. Given the cost, most students are not paying for their own education. The attitudes college administrators take toward first-year students is, "you're all grown up," but they

are not. Most college students are just kids who were living at home before college and may be returning home after the year is over. They don't need hand-holding, but they do need a structure and perhaps a mentor who looks out for them.[34]

Dr. Benjamin believes that meetings with psychological counselors should not be at the discretion of the student but rather should be better integrated into the college experience, at least for first-year students.[35] Just as appointments with academic counselors are built in to the academic calendar, perhaps social and mental health counseling should be a part of a student's schedule. University-sponsored support groups led by trained professionals may be another ideal available someday. Until this happens, parents need to know that as caring as the school seems, there may be no one to call but your son or daughter to find out how your child is doing.

HEALTH INSURANCE

While your child is still healthy, it is a good idea to find out what your insurance covers—and whether it covers your college student at all.

By some estimates, only two-thirds of college students are covered under their parents' health insurance or a university plan.[36] This leaves a full one-third of U.S. college students without any health insurance. For those who do have insurance, many have too little coverage or do not know how to access their care providers. Confusing provider rules, deductibles and copayments that vary according to the services used, and contractual legalese are just some of the challenges students must overcome before receiving medical care.

Parents and college-bound students should carefully investigate whether the student is covered by the family health insurance plan while away at college. Dr. Benjamin, the pediatrician, warns that many health care companies set age limits on coverage for children under a family health plan to control their costs.[37] With the college years emotionally and physically straining, the health risks to students are considerable. According to William DeJong, Ph.D., of the

U.S. Department of Education's Higher Education Center for Alcohol and Other Drug Prevention, college is an especially hard time for students as they tend to travel a great deal and engage in more high-risk activity than their younger peers.[38] The ready availability of alcohol tends to further exacerbate the situation. As a result, many colleges require students to obtain health insurance in order to attend.

The big question is how much insurance should the student purchase? According to the American College Health Association, students should find a plan that provides at least $50,000 of medical coverage.[39] Regional variation in health care costs should also be considered in selecting a plan for your child with costs generally higher in the northeastern United States.

Even when a college-age child is eligible for coverage under a parent's plan, the parents and their college-bound students need to explore their options carefully. Given the size of their groups and their superior negotiating position, some colleges may be able to offer better health care plans for students and staff than those available though a parent's employer.

A smart school carefully monitors use of its student health insurance plan. A few years back, the University of Oregon did the numbers and found that relatively few students were taking advantage of the student health plan because of its high deductible. Armed with data showing that 95 percent of the university's students had yearly medical costs of less than $200 (the old deductible), the school was able to negotiate a new plan with its provider that charged students a $40 flat fee each semester.

STUDENT HEALTH SERVICES

Student health services are commonly available to students in order to provide them with primary medical and nursing care, mental health services, and preventive care. Though much maligned, student health services are typically well run and provide excellent care to those they serve. Dr. Eric Rubin, the infectious disease specialist, has found that in Boston, at least, the quality of student health services is excellent.

Hours can, however, be a problem, especially for smaller health services that do not offer services around the clock. Most colleges and universities have created brochures that describe the operation of the student health services as well as the coverage available under the student health insurance plan available at the school. Before moving to campus, students and parents may want to review these materials for information on how health services work.

Unfortunately, many colleges and universities do not provide blanket medical coverage to students. Parents and students alike will be interested to learn as well that the quality of student health services varies greatly from university to university. At its best, student health services can be a useful, supportive, and welcome place that students can turn to with health problems and concerns. At worst, they can be poorly staffed programs with second-rate health professionals racing against the clock and a tight budget to serve a population well beyond their capacity.

Although much of the focus of student health services is on women's health, a growing number of colleges and universities are creating men's health clinics to better address the health concerns of college men. According to a July 7, 2000, article in the *Chronicle of Higher Education,* the University of Colorado at Boulder, San Francisco State University, Tulane University, Florida International University, and the University of Pennsylvania will all have men's health centers by September 2001.[40]

With many college-age men indifferent about their health, some critics think the male-only clinics are a fad and question whether they will get used. While many healthy college men do not require much more than good health information, ailments commonly experienced by college men include broken bones, STDs, and urinary tract problems. At many colleges, STD testing represents the lion's share of the male student cases that come into the student health clinic. Just why college men need a good health clinic is no surprise to those who work in student health. According to one physician interviewed for the *Chronicle* article,

There is no better place for a men's clinic than a college campus. "I don't mean to paint a picture that all college students have multiple partners every night, but the 18-to-34-year-old age group will have significantly more partners than the 35-to-60-year-old age group."[41]

Male college students are said to be more likely than their female counterparts to engage in high-risk drinking and risky sexual behavior, to sexually assault someone, or to attempt suicide. Additionally, because of their age, college students are better candidates for preventive medicine aimed at cutting the risks of heart disease, prostate cancer, and other medical concerns affecting older persons.

Since not every college man has a special clinic at his disposal, parents and their sons may want to add a full physical to the to-do list before their sons leave for college. A physician should take the time to ask the right questions and bring up matters a young man may not be prepared to ask such as how to do a self-exam for signs of testicular cancer. Although Lance Armstrong's recent book and victory in the Tour de France bicycle race have certainly raised awareness of the risk of testicular cancer, many college men still feel immune to this and many other health risks such as overeating, depression, unprotected sex, smoking, steroid use, and illicit drug use. At a minimum, you should encourage your children to seek regular checkups.

THE RIGHT TO PRIVACY IN STUDENT MEDICAL RECORDS

Parents concerned about their child's health and well-being may find college and university policies involving a student's right to privacy completely baffling and nerve-wracking. In accordance with state and federal privacy laws and the confidentiality policies of most student health and counseling centers, these centers won't release health information about a student without the student's formal, signed consent. An exception to this rule is life-threatening circumstances. According to law professor Peter Lake, coauthor of *The Rights and*

Responsibilities of the Modern University: Who Assumes the Risks of College Life? "In general the confidentiality of a college student's health records has to be balanced against the need for specific individuals to know that information."[42]

Although difficult for some parents to accept, these laws and policies are good in that they guarantee your adult son or daughter the cherished right to privacy, thereby encouraging students to seek the care they need. Embarrassment and fear of a parent's reaction to a health problem would likely drive many students away from the student health services. By assuring students that their trip to the clinic for treatment, say, of an STD will remain private, students will more likely seek help for their health problems.

Parents who need or want to know about their child's health care while at college should ask their son or daughter in a way that is not threatening to the child. A son or daughter who fears being punished or sanctioned by a parent for contracting a sexually transmitted disease is, in my view, correct in keeping that information from the parent. Parents of female students should also know that the same policy will apply to the health records of a student who shows up at health services thinking she is pregnant.

Regrettably, every year thousands of health professionals are thrust into the unenviable position of counseling a student whose pregnancy was either unwanted or unexpected or both. In an interview with me in December 2000, Jonathan Bertman, M.D., a clinical assistant professor of family medicine at Brown University, explained that unwanted pregnancies are a significant problem seen all too frequently in his practice in Hope Valley, Rhode Island. According to Dr. Bertman,

> Well-meaning parents all too often make the mistaken assumption that providing their child with contraception will be misinterpreted as a license to engage in unbridled sexual activity. Those students who have easy access to contraception and condoms are not any more sexually active than their unprotected peers, they just get pregnant and STDs less often.[43]

The spring 2000 suicide of a nineteen-year-old MIT student, the third at that school in that year, also raised many difficult legal and ethical questions surrounding student privacy rights versus the parental right to know about their child's well-being. In its defense in what is becoming another very public affair for MIT, school administrators have underscored that the student did not want her parents involved. As a result the school is reviewing whether administrators and staff should specifically counter the wishes of individual students.

Given the outcome here, the answer seems clear. In a May 21, 2000, interview with the *Boston Globe,* Cho Hyun, the student's father, said, "If parents are kept blind because of no communication between the school and parents, and the school's not doing a full-fledged job of taking care of students, then there's a chance of an instance like this repeating."[44]

While I am a firm supporter of students' right to privacy, the position of a parent mourning the loss of his daughter is quite understandable.

COUNSELING SERVICES

Unfortunately, college psychological counseling services are often not of the highest quality. Elissa Grad, a former consultant with Work Family Directions, an employee assistance advisory program in Boston, relates how frequently she received calls from parents seeking advice on the availability of mental health services in a son's or daughter's college community. Grad recalls how shocked she was initially to learn just how limited student psychological counseling services were on many campuses and how ill-prepared many residence hall assistants (RAs) were to handle mental health problems. Training and support for these frontline workers are simply inadequate. In general, Grad found the universities with which she dealt better equipped to diagnose and provide services to a student with learning disabilities than to one in need of mental health services.[45]

Indeed, according to Sylvia Epstein, Ph.D., a psychologist specializing in evaluation and assessment in Scarsdale, New York, many college students are not diagnosed with a learning disability until college.[46]

Counseling centers tend to be at their best when they are providing static health information to students. Many counseling programs, such as the program at Washington State University, have set up resource rooms with information on specific topics and a small library of videotapes that students may view in the center. A sampling of the audio- and videotapes available at the University of Washington counseling service library cover such topics as eating disorders, depression, and stress management.

As parents concerned about our son's or daughter's health and well-being, we should not stand by waiting for the colleges and universities to do a better job of educating them about their health. By starting your child off right regarding his or her health, nutrition, and sexuality, you will be helping your son or daughter to achieve independence and full-fledged individual responsibility. Lastly, in talking with your college-bound student about these issues, be sure to teach him or her to seek help when needed.

SEVEN

Safe and Sound

◘ ◘ ◘

Let's get things straight. College campuses are still generally safer places to live than most American cities. Even the much maligned schools—the rust belt urban campuses often portrayed in the media as islands in a sea of crime—are on the whole safe places for your child to live and study. With campus safety such a primary concern for parents and students, most campuses, including urban schools in cities with high crime rates, spend a substantial percentage of their budget keeping things safe.[1]

On campus and in surrounding communities, the signs of this concern abound. When visiting prospective schools, alert parents and students will note the college's focus on safety in the form of call boxes, campus escort services, evening bus services, closed-circuit televisions, electronic card access systems, and crime awareness training for students, as well as tried-and-true crime prevention strategies like campus police and security patrols. And these are just the most obvious approaches the nation's colleges are taking to protect your child. Security checks on faculty, staff, and, yes, students, are increasingly common on large and small campuses alike. While prospective students during an initial campus tour generally focus on getting a feel for the campus and sizing up whether they will fit in, parents' concerns tend to focus on campus safety, academic quality, and cost.

So if campuses are generally safe, why is campus crime such a prominent concern of parents of college-bound students? First and foremost, because it is *your* child we are talking about. There are, of course, other reasons as well. The already-mentioned media takes much of the credit, but so does the work of media-savvy campus security advocacy groups like Security on Campus—Howard and Connie Clery's memorial to their daughter Jeanne, a student slain in a brutal attack at Lehigh University in the late 1980s. The Clerys and their allies have been the prime movers in the legislative arena as well, advancing federal legislation aimed at improving the accuracy of campus crime reporting statistics so that students (and their parents) can make a more informed decision about the school they will be attending.

Largely as a result of the Clerys' efforts, in October 2000, the U.S. Department of Education's Office of Postsecondary Education launched a Web site that is supposed to feature campus crime statistics for the nation's more than six thousand colleges and universities. The Web site, http://ope.ed.gov/security, was officially authorized by Congress with passage of the 1998 Amendments to the Higher Education Act. The colleges' requirement to publicly disclose these statistics is referred to as the Clery Act, which will be described in full in the following pages.

While the U.S. Department of Education's effort to gather this data is indeed laudable, some campus safety advocates, including yours truly, complain that it is still difficult to make comparisons between colleges because of the disparate methods schools and the college communities use to compile crime data. Additionally, as the Department of Education is quick to concede, it does not confirm that the figures the campuses are reporting are accurate.

Other groups that deserve credit for heightening campus crime awareness include the grass-roots acquaintance rape and sexual assault victim advocacy movements. Resource centers like the U.S. Department of Education's Higher Education Center for Alcohol and Other Drug Prevention have done their part as well. The Higher Education Center—the nation's primary resource for colleges and universities on alcohol, drug, and violence issues—is operated by Health and Human Development Programs, a division of the nonprofit Education Development Center, Inc., of Newton, Massachusetts. Both the victim advocacy and prevention constituencies have helped raise public awareness that not all campus crime and violence can be blamed on the campus outsider. Indeed, a good deal of crime on campus, as in the community at large, involves acquaintances who may have been heavily intoxicated or stoned.

Litigation is another important factor in raising consciousness about campus crime. Cases such as the civil and criminal suits filed in response to the 1992 Simon's Rock College of Bard incident, in which campus administrators appear to have been negligent in handling a student prone to extremist views and violence, have exposed for the public just how wrong things can go on a campus. Just hours before student Wayne Lo went on a shooting spree killing two and wounding four others, Lo had met with and convinced the dean of students that a package Lo had received from a mail-order firearms store *did not* contain a gun or ammunition. Of course the package *did* contain the bullets Lo used to kill and injure others later that evening. Moreover, even before Lo's UPS package from the arms company had arrived at the college receptionist's desk, college administrators were concerned about Lo, whom they knew to be an emotionally troubled eighteen-year-old prone to homophobic and other extremist positions. *GoneBoy: A Walkabout*, a 1999 book by Gregory Gibson, is an eloquent memorial to Galen Gibson, the author's son and one of the men killed in the Simon's Rock College of Bard shootings.

Admittedly, colleges are in a difficult spot, needing to balance the privacy rights of students, faculty, and staff against legitimate campus safety concerns. In light of incidents like the shootings at Simon's Rock College of Bard and the late-1990s murder of a Harvard student by her roommate, colleges can no longer claim that such events are unforeseeable aberrations. Hopefully, as more parents become aware of the colleges' dirty little secrets, more colleges will pay closer attention to danger from within and to getting help for those who may be suffering from delusional or otherwise dangerous thoughts about their classmates or the world.

Given the heightened perception of campus crime problems and the flurry of litigation in recent years, colleges across the country have recognized the need to respond meaningfully to parental concerns about campus safety. But how dangerous are the nation's campuses really? And are colleges taking the right steps to respond to the kinds of crime that may, or may not, plague their campuses? Although much of the parental focus on campus safety has been on crimes of violence, most campus crime involves lesser crimes, like theft of personal property. As noted in chapter 3, laptops and other small electronic devices, as well as cash and credit cards, are the prime targets of campus criminals—be they students or strangers. Many colleges have installed card access systems in an effort to improve residence hall security, but that hardly helps tackle problems from within, including theft and related crime by fellow students, staff, and, *yes,* faculty.

In principle, compliance with the Clery Act should be far more than just a data collection exercise for the colleges. Compliance with the act *can* help campuses to better understand crime and violence at and around their institutions. By using the information to inform their prevention efforts and modify campus policy, colleges can improve their response to campus community crime and violence generally.

As are most colleges, Lewis & Clark College is concerned about the safety and welfare of all campus members and guests and is committed to promoting a safe and secure campus environment. Acknowledging that no campus can totally isolate itself from crime, Lewis & Clark has developed a series of policies and procedures designed to ensure that every possible precaution is taken to protect the campus community. But the college has not stopped there. Lewis & Clark also hired the nonprofit National Center for Higher Education Risk Management (NCHERM) to conduct an audit of Lewis & Clark's Clery Act compliance.[2] While acknowledging that NCHERM's assessment is not a legal guarantee that the college is in compliance with the act, the college's use of the independent organization reflects the school's commitment to making sure its policies are as good as they can be and as great an aid to campus safety as possible.

According to S. Daniel Carter, vice president of Security on Campus, keeping your son or daughter safe at school involves making him or her aware of the risks and steps he or she can take to protect against them.[3] Carter says, "Most college campuses seem far too idyllic to play host to crime. But they do, for a number of reasons." Demographics are one factor. According to the U.S. Department of Justice, eighteen- to twenty-five-year-olds are most likely to commit or be victimized by crime. College students tend to live crammed together, often under stressful conditions. Heavy drinking and illicit drug use do not improve students' judgment either.

To help keep your child safe, safety advocates recommend that parents encourage their child to do the following:

- Decline to have his or her photo taken and personal information published (especially true for women) for distribution to the campus community. Fraternities and other student groups have been known to use a new student's photo and listing to call up and sexually harass first-year students.
- Study the campus and the surrounding neighborhood so that he or she knows a few different routes between the residence hall and the classrooms. Encouraging your child to memorize the location of campus emergency call boxes is another good idea.
- Share schedules and anticipated whereabouts with a few close friends and create informal and formal buddy systems when going out or traveling at night.
- Walk with friends or take the campus shuttle or escort service at night. Parents can reinforce that if it is necessary to walk alone at night, the student should use only well-lit main routes rather than shortcuts through alleys and entrances. (Groups like Security on Campus and the National Center for Higher Education Risk Management advise parents to complain if the campus is not lit well enough at night.)
- Steer clear of people who are drunk or high, whether they are alone or in groups.

- Always lock the doors and windows at night. Your son or
  daughter should not have to compromise his or her safety
  to accommodate an irresponsible roommate who has lost a
  key or access card.

Some other common campus safety suggestions compiled by
Security on Campus include encouraging your child to do the
following:

- Program his or her phone's speed dial with emergency numbers, including the campus police, your number, and some
  nearby friends' numbers.
- Change the lock to his or her dorm room if the keys or access
  card is lost.
- Close dorm entrances that are left or propped open for con-
  venience or through another's negligence.
- (For those who live off-campus) contact the student legal aid
  representative to draft a lease that stipulates minimum standards of security and responsibility.[4]

Cathy Kirshner, a Great Neck, New York, mother of a Harvard
University senior and a Syracuse University freshman, stresses with
her daughter and son the commonsense safety issues they may not
have taken into account while living at home.[5] For example, when
her daughter left for college, Kirshner cautioned her not to take
showers in the afternoon when her co-ed dormitory tended to be de-
serted. Instead, she advised her to use the common shower area in
the evenings or mornings when many other students were around.
Sometimes, parents tend to forget to offer their college-bound son or
daughter the little commonsense recommendations that may prove
the most helpful.

Although campus crime statistics remain notoriously unreliable,
students and parents may also want to read the college's annual campus crime reports, watch for coverage of campus crime in the school
newspaper, and consult local police or neighborhood associations to
learn about local and campus crime problems.

THE CLERY ACT

Assuming that you are still reading this chapter instead of turning to another one that is more pleasant, some history is probably in order. The U.S. Congress passed the Student Right-to-Know and Campus Security Act (20 U.S.C., section 1092) in 1990 to require colleges and universities to publicly disclose crime statistics and crime prevention and security policies and procedures on campus. The law was amended again in 1992 to require that schools afford victims specific basic rights and again in 1998 to include additional reporting obligations. As a memorial to Jeanne Clery, a murdered Lehigh University student, the 1998 amendments changed the name of the legislation to the Clery Act.

Contrary to the statutory mandate, colleges vary widely in their crime data collection and reporting procedures. In a 1997 study, the Government Accounting Office found that colleges have had difficulty in consistently interpreting and applying the Campus Security Act's reporting requirements, including how they decide which incidents to include in their reports, how to classify crimes, how to include incidents reported to campus officials rather than to law enforcement officers, how to interpret federal requirements for reporting sexual offenses, and how to report data on hate crimes.

Campus crimes, particularly those involving students, point up the tension between the dean of students' legal obligation to report a crime to public authorities and his or her role as a public relations manager and booster for the school. Some of my own research suggests that thousands of criminal offenses pass through campus courts each year rather than through public criminal courts, though meaningful data on actual levels of campus crime are not available.

Despite some colleges' half-hearted compliance with the Clery Act, as of January 2001, the U.S. Department of Education has fined only one college for failing to comply with the act. In 2000, Mount Saint Clare College in Iowa was ordered to pay $25,000 for (1) not adequately disclosing its crime statistics, (2) failing to provide campus security reports to prospective students and employees, and (3) providing incomplete information about campus security policies.

Why has there been so little action taken to enforce stricter compliance? Well, mostly it is because of the lack of Education Department staff and resources to investigate lax reporting by some colleges. A victim and target of partisan legislative squabbling, the Education Department has been largely gutted in recent years, leaving staff who remain hard-pressed to do all the work they have to do. Campus safety advocacy groups like Security on Campus welcome the action against Mount Saint Clare College and hope that it is the beginning of a trend toward more aggressive enforcement of the law.

PUTTING THE SPIN ON CAMPUS CRIME

When I was young and impressionable, my mother taught me how to read the newspaper. Though we were blessed with an unusually good paper—the *New York Times*—even reading the *Times* required caution. The news was filled, Mom warned, with trial balloons—stories created by skilled press agents and pawned off on unsuspecting and even fully cognizant reporters—as "news." What I now know to be wishful thinking, or worse, lies, often appeared as news throughout the paper. Today's Internet with its real and fabricated "truth" had nothing on the old pros—the communications directors—who could spin a story as easy as pie. Well, the same must be said about some of those charged with reporting campus crime data. (My sincere apologies to the many honest directors of campus police and security out there.)

Even the critics appreciate that campus crime reporting is no easy business. Speaking of compliance with the Clery Act, S. Daniel Carter of Security on Campus cautions, "The diversity of compliance is going to be so extensive, it's going to be hard to make comparisons."[6] The challenge of including crimes committed on land adjacent to a campus that is "reasonably contiguous" public property is the least of the college's—and consequently your—problems. According to the U.S. Department of Education, the effort to accurately report campus crimes should involve a "good faith" effort by the campus to collect information from local police. While colleges that are found to be in noncompliance with the crime-reporting law face fines of up to $25,000, as with the law generally, the hard part remains making a case against a school that has not made a good faith effort.

The Clery Act is, of course, not the only federal legislative initiative aimed at better informing parents and students of the state of campus safety. From time to time, particularly in election years, some in Congress like to push legislation aimed at requiring colleges to better track sex offenders and other students perceived as posing a threat to the public safety. In June 2000, the U.S. House of Representatives unanimously approved a bill that would require colleges to make known on their campuses the identities of students and employees who are "registered sex offenders." To the bill's supporters, the sex-offender provision would help alert college women to the presence of "sex offenders or rapists" on the campus. To others, however, the legislative proposal is a misguided measure that would create hysteria as well as unduly burden the colleges and universities charged with making known the identify of registered sex offenders on their campus. In a June 2000 article in the *Chronicle of Higher Education,* critics argue, "Colleges would have to match their databases of employees and students against those of the states in which these individuals have lived. This would be a special challenge, they said, for colleges that enroll students from all over the country."[7]

"Greater awareness of potential security risks on campus" versus "undue administrative and financial burden on colleges and universities that will add nothing in the way of security" are the two poles of the debate. In case my position on this particular legislative proposal is not already clear, I will reiterate that I believe it is a red herring detracting colleges and universities from the challenge of making campuses safer places for students and staff to live, study, and work. There are far more effective ways to make campuses safer places, and this book and the resources I describe in the "Resources" chapter are sources for them.

SEXUAL OFFENSES

Rape and sexual assault cases appear to present a particularly difficult issue for campuses. For a variety of reasons, not the least of which is the bad PR for the campus, many colleges just cannot seem to define terms such as "campus," "student," and "sexual assault" for the sake of the college's crime reporting. Schools tend to get stuck, for example, when considering whether the sexual assault of a student by another student at an off-campus facility should be included in campus crime statistics. Or should the sexual assault of a student that occurred on campus but during spring break be included? In addition, reporting categories may differ to conform to state-crime classifications or other classification schema, rather than conforming to categories mandated by federal law.

According to Michael Clay Smith, an expert on campus rape and sexual assault, colleges need to redouble their efforts and do as follows:

- inform students of the danger of both acquaintance and stranger rape
- provide students with a safe and secure living environment
- demonstrate a commitment to the vigorous prosecution of rape and other crimes that occur on campus[8]

ALCOHOL AND DRUG VIOLATIONS

Whatever your view of underage drinking and illicit drug use, the fact is, colleges are focusing more than they have in prior decades on enforcement of drinking and illicit drug laws. According to a June 2000 article in the *Chronicle of Higher Education,* an annual *Chronicle* survey of campus crime revealed the following:

Alcohol arrests at American colleges rose 24.3 percent in 1998, the largest increase in seven years, while arrests for violations of drug laws grew at their sharpest rate in three years, increasing 11.1 percent. This marks the seventh consecutive year that arrests for liquor- and narcotics-law violations have gone up.[9]

What explains these increases? Has student drinking and drug use increased in recent years? Has the Clery Act requirement that schools report crime beyond the campus made the difference? Or is it just that enforcement has increased? How is a parent to interpret the data and judge a school's response?

Perhaps over time the numbers will generate more accurate pictures of campus crime, but for now, it seems to me few conclusions can be drawn from the data other than that there is an increase in the perceived risk of arrest for underage drinking or illicit drug use. To the extent that perception is reality, you would do well to gently warn your son or daughter. Reviewing the *Chronicle*'s crime survey on the way to a campus visit might not be a half-bad idea. The annual survey is based on the most recent statistics that colleges and universities are required by federal law to disclose. The survey is based on the responses of 481 four-year institutions, each enrolling at least 5,000 students. Community colleges—schools that are largely commuter campuses and typically do not experience as many crimes as do four-year institutions—are not included in the survey.

HATE CRIMES ON CAMPUS

As with the discussion of campus crime and safety generally, there is always the risk of overstating a problem. That said, law enforcement agencies and groups that monitor such activity have noted a modest increase in campus hate or bias crime. With frightful accuracy to an actual occurrence, *Followers,* an independent film released during the spring of 2000 depicts a "nigger night" at a New Jersey university.[10] Other real incidents from the late 1990s include the following:

- Several historically black colleges received racist mail and bomb threats as students returned to campus.[11]

- Sixty Asian American students at UC-Irvine received death threats through e-mail before the start of the school year.[12]
- A female African American student at Brown University is alleged to have been physically assaulted and called a "statistic" by several white classmates.[13]

College life has changed. The antisweatshop strikes are not the only thing keeping some students busy this academic year. Parents should know that some hate groups take advantage of the open environment of many universities to recruit naïve young people to their twisted ways of thinking. These groups exploit opportunities at colleges that pride themselves on being bastions of open dialogue, using the campus as a soapbox to recruit and rouse alienated and often paranoid young people to cockamamy ideas such as the white race is being crowded out by other ethnic groups.

It was a deadly rampage in Illinois and Indiana in 1999 by a racist and anti-Semitic former college student that caused some smarter colleges to finally face the music. For student affairs personnel at these schools, the killings definitively underscored the need for colleges and universities to develop constitutionally valid strategies for identifying and making the public aware of dangerous students in their midst. The Midwest rampage, resulting in two deaths and the shooting of at least nine others, raised the question, what can institutions do to avoid being used as cover for dangerous organizations and individuals who hide behind the veil of privacy laws and student confidentiality policies? Following a thorough review of its admissions policy, Indiana University, which had accepted the killer—a University of Illinois transfer student—revised its transfer policy to make it easier to identify dangerous students. According to a July 3, 2000, article in the *Indiana Daily Student,* starting in fall 2001, Indiana will require all freshmen and transfer students to provide information about any criminal convictions on their admissions forms.[14] This question was previously voluntary. Indiana's code of ethics has also been changed to allow the university to dismiss students who lie on their applications. The *Indiana Daily Student* article quotes Indiana

University Trustee Ray Richardson in a startlingly candid admission as saying, "Someone was murdered because we didn't have this rule."[15] Most other Big Ten schools already have this policy in place.

I recite the known facts because it really is just absurd that this incident was not prevented from occurring. The student came to the attention of the University of Illinois police when, in a single week in October 1997, he was accused of beating up his girlfriend and fighting with other students. Concerned about his behavior and his reputation in the college community of Urbana-Champaign as an avowed racist and extremist, University of Illinois administrators met with the student and his parents and permitted him to withdraw without penalty. By summer 1998, he was enrolled at Indiana University, espousing the same inflammatory racist and anti-Semitic views he had expressed at Illinois. It is not known what the Indiana admissions office knew of his past at Illinois and how effectively its application screened for information that might have uncovered his antisocial views and history of domestic violence. However, you would think that if the admissions office had been aware of this information, it might have looked elsewhere to fill its college's classes.

Parents need to know that, while colleges do care about hate crimes, their words often fall short of the substantive change that has now occurred, too late to save the lives that have been lost, at Indiana. Typical of the affirmative stand many colleges are taking against hate crime is the statement issued by Binghamton University of the State University of New York. Binghamton addressed hate crimes in its Rules of Student Conduct, which are printed in the university's student handbook. The handbook is given to each student, and it is also published in its entirety on the university's Web site. Under "Procedures for Review of Student Conduct" (section F, Sanctions), the following paragraph is included:

> Any student found responsible for a violation or attempted violation of the Rules of Student Conduct who has targeted a person or group because of race, color, sex, sexual orientation, transgendered status, religion, age, disability, veteran status,

marital status, national origin, or ancestry may be subject to a more severe sanction than would ordinarily accompany that violation or attempted violation.[16]

Schools that take the time to create antibias policies now need to take steps against those who violate those policies. From interviews with students and administrators across the country, I know that some schools are not doing all that they can to enforce their stated goals. If not, I ask rhetorically, what is the point of having the policy?

Parents and prospective college students should keep in mind that campus crimes, particularly those involving students, point up the tension between the legal obligation of the dean of students to report a crime to public authorities and his or her role as a public relations manager and booster for the school. According to a May 6, 1996, article by Nina Bernstein in the *New York Times,* and some of my own research, thousands of criminal offenses pass through campus courts each year rather than through public criminal courts.[17] Lastly, many schools continue to accord students alleged to have committed crimes "kid-glove" handling in quasi-judicial confidential proceedings.

CAMPUS "JUSTICE"

College disciplinary systems were originally intended to deal with infractions that were neither felonies nor misdemeanors. According to John Silber, the combative former president of Boston University, writing in a May 9, 1996, editorial in the *New York Times,* "Most campus disciplinary systems do not have the basics required for a fair trial: a professional and independent judiciary, enforceable rules of procedure, and effective and fairly applied sanctions." Although most college and university attorneys and campus judicial system staff would have you believe otherwise, these quasi-judicial systems are under attack.

In Massachusetts, a case brought against Brandeis University by former student David Schaer created quite a stir and went all the way to the Massachusetts Supreme Judicial Court, the commonwealth's highest court. The ruling by a very divided court upheld Brandeis's judicial proceedings but raised many questions as well. What might have been a widely cited decision supporting the sanctity of college disciplinary systems will likely instead cause more colleges to go even further than they already have gone in honoring the rights of accused students. According to lawyer Bradley M. Henry of the Boston law firm of Meehan, Boyle, and Cohen, P.C., "The insistence with which colleges had until this case maintained that they are a protected place is incomprehensible in this day and age."[18]

Under attack from both crime victims disappointed with the meting out of light sanctions and accused students who feel their due process rights have been violated, the college disciplinary model is widely viewed as overdue for a major overhaul by higher education legal scholars and laypersons alike. Indeed, the only ones who appear to be holding out are those who operate the systems and swear by their efficacy.

Despite the widespread criticism that these procedures do not offer the basics required of a fair trial, many colleges continue to pursue criminal matters, including allegations of rape and sexual assault, through their campus disciplinary systems rather than referring them to public authorities. In some communities, the relationship between "gown" and "town" is so closely wound that the college holds undue sway, influencing which criminal cases involving students, if any, are publicly adjudicated. Elsewhere, a school's perceived need to continue to collect tuition from the accused student and to keep that student enrolled in good standing appears to interfere with the need to take meaningful legal or disciplinary action against the student. Many schools use the veil of confidentiality to protect themselves and their public image rather than to protect victims and the accused.

In her 1996 article in the *New York Times*, journalist Nina Bernstein describes one such disciplinary system as follows:

> No one was supposed to know that John Higdon almost died that night three years ago—not the national office of the fraternity that nearly killed him, not the University of Georgia,

where he was a student, nor his parents, and certainly not the public. But after a hazing ritual left the 19-year-old pledge too drunk to breathe, a nurse who helped save his life broke hospital rules and called his mother. Four days later, a Georgia Supreme Court ruling opened the university's secret student court to public scrutiny. And within weeks, what would have been a closed-door disciplinary hearing about the near-fatal incident was thrown into the public spotlight.[19]

Bernstein's article goes on to describe how the case remains a rare window on the protected place that fraternities occupy at the heart of the campus justice system in operation at colleges throughout the country.

Heather Karjane, the project director for a U.S. Department of Justice study of sexual assault prevention programs on college campuses notes similar problems in the handling of rape cases by some colleges. In an interview in January 2001, Karjane noted several studies that have estimated that only one in a hundred campus rapes gets reported to the police. Among the reasons noted for students failing to report their victimization are their wish to avoid embarrassment, concern that the victim will receive unsympathetic treatment from police and courts, fear of reprisal by the rapist, and lack of confidence that the police can apprehend the perpetrator.[20]

To the embarrassment of the academic community, which often bristles at such criticism, the need for new methods of dealing with campus crime involving students and staff is confirmed on almost a daily basis. From the Ivy League and Big Ten schools to the nation's lesser-known private four-year colleges, administrators are finding themselves increasingly plagued by a campus judicial or disciplinary system that has not kept pace with the nature of campus crime. In practice, this may mean that prosecutors and publicly sworn law enforcement officers are being kept in the dark about campus crimes or crimes involving a student. Moreover, the order in which the campus and public judicial system cases are pursued has particularly important implications. For example, when campus proceedings are conducted first, both the accused and crime victims may be at risk.

Information they provide in good faith efforts to comply with quasi-judicial proceedings may prejudice them in subsequent public proceedings.

Confirming much of what Bernstein of the *New York Times* found in 1996, a May 10, 2000, exposé in the *Los Angeles Times* notes the following:

> With reports of misconduct on the rise at many California colleges and universities, campus judicial systems are quietly handling thousands of cases each year ranging from plagiarism and petty larceny to physical assault and rape.
>
> Drunken Pomona College students went joyriding in the dean's golf cart. Chico State dorm residents were nabbed in a drug sting. A pair of UC Santa Cruz students, dubbed Bonnie and Clyde, were arrested for two armed robberies. When students are accused of such offenses, the stakes are high because costly educations, careers and school reputations are hanging in the balance. In some cases, students hire lawyers—and one enlisted a handwriting expert—for campus disciplinary hearings.
>
> To mete out punishments, virtually every school uses a quasi-judicial arm that convenes behind closed doors. Students and faculty who have little legal training serve as investigators, prosecutors and judges. They usually operate independent of police and courts, and seldom refer cases for criminal action.[21]

Michelle A. Goldfarb, director of the Office of Student Conduct at the University of Pennsylvania, is realistic about the fact that there will never be a perfect campus or public judicial system response to cases involving so-called acquaintance rape:

> From a victim and student conduct director's standpoint, these cases are at best imperfect. They require the victim to go through a great deal of trauma, and, however respectful the campus judicial system, the victim's privacy is often compromised by the campus newspaper or some other means.[22]

As a former public prosecutor, Goldfarb feels that Penn's system is effectively handling such cases and believes that most victims find the process much less burdensome emotionally than a public criminal prosecution. Nonetheless, Goldfarb would love to see a still more straightforward disciplinary system model, and this is what she has sought to implement at Penn.

The *Los Angeles Times* exposé quotes J. Lance Gilmer, an unusually candid director of student conduct at the University of California–Riverside as saying:

> There is no doubt that colleges are underreporting crimes, especially rape. . . . Like everyone, I used to view colleges as safe havens. I never thought about people . . . raping, assaulting, or fighting. I never thought that existed here. The myth I had been living under was just that. A myth.[23]

In private, judicial board members at many schools will admit that they know of alleged rape cases that were not handled by the boards and therefore did not show up in the college's campus crime statistics.

The media's role in blowing the cover on the quasi-judicial nature of campus judicial proceedings cannot be overstated. Mark Goodman of the Student Press Law Center in Virginia notes, "It was only when these bodies started dealing with more serious crimes that people became interested."[24] The Student Press Law Center is a nonprofit group that advocates increased public disclosure of student judicial proceedings. The group was very involved in the Christy Brzonkala litigation, a 1995 case involving a gang rape at Virginia Tech that went all the way to the U.S. Supreme Court.

INADEQUATELY TRAINED HEARING OFFICERS

One of the most common, though startling, criticisms of campus judicial systems is that student judicial system staff training is often woefully inadequate given the difficult decisions that staff—often upper-class or graduate students—are called upon to make. Many colleges still do not routinely refer cases that are indeed criminal to local police for investigation. Instead, various college staff advise student crime victims that they *may* want to consider pressing criminal charges. As a result, the adjudication of criminal allegations, including those of rape, may end up before a judicial board staffed by students, professors, and college administrators with relatively little training or experience with legal matters. As a sort of check on unreasonable behavior by the judicial boards, a college dean or other senior college administrator often serves as a final reviewer of the boards' rulings.

The *Los Angeles Times* article describes proceedings at Chico State this way, "Members of the school panels receive little training in how to assess evidence. Most panels only study the student conduct code. At Pomona, the training consists of a day's lecture by an attorney about using the 'Socratic method' to seek the truth."[25]

With largely untrained nonlawyers running the process, many judicial boards do not let lawyers argue on behalf of the students. Lawyers are sometimes allowed to attend judicial hearings as advisors.

Parents and students who become familiar with college judicial proceedings are often surprised to learn how little predictability there may be in the meting out of sanctions. What may warrant a student's expulsion or suspension at one college may result in little more than a slap on the wrist at another.

TOUGH QUESTIONS ON CAMPUS DISCIPLINE

While working on a research project concerning college disciplinary systems in the late 1990s, I developed a list of questions that may interest parents and prospective students as well. Consider asking these types of questions when you visit a college:

- What procedures do the campus disciplinary systems and public courts use to facilitate communication and coordination?
- What campus mechanisms are available for enforcing court orders (orders of protection)?
- What mechanisms are in place to prevent local colleges from meddling in public judicial proceedings involving students charged with serious offenses?
- What mechanisms have the colleges developed to deal with widespread problems such as acquaintance rape, drug dealing, driving while intoxicated, drinking and drug use by (underage) students at on-campus and off-campus school-sanctioned functions?

Additionally, the group Security on Campus advises parents and prospective students to ask college admissions officers and the dean of students such questions as:

- Does the institution publish campus crime information as required by the Clery Act? (Request a copy.)
- Do the annual crime statistics include reports to the dean's office, judicial hearings, and women's rape/crisis centers?
- Are security logs open for public inspection?
- Does the school ask applicants if they have been arrested and convicted of a crime?
- Are campus crime policies and penalties explicitly addressed during orientation, as well as clearly stated in the student handbook?
- Are drinking, drug, and weapon laws strictly enforced?
- Are single sex and "substance free" dormitories available?
- Does the school address the entire student body during the academic year about growing problems related to campus crime: date rape and sexual assault, alcohol and drug abuse, and sexually transmitted diseases? When? Who addresses the students?

- Does the school have an open judicial committee? How many and what type of cases did the judicial committee handle last year?
- Does the school provide immediate medical, psychological, and legal aid to victims, as required by the federal Campus Sexual Assault Victim's Bill of Rights?[26]

Security on Campus recommends that you pose similar questions to the campus security department and the rape crisis center and then compare the responses. If, after you have posed these questions to several groups on campus, your son or daughter is accepted to the school—Congratulations!—and welcome to Fort Knox!

EIGHT

Who's Responsible?

◨ ◨ ◨

SCOTT KRUEGER AND THE CASE AGAINST MIT

In 1997, the Massachusetts Institute of Technology went from bastion of the brilliant to out-of-control "party central." The alcohol poisoning death of Scott Krueger, a young man of infinite promise, cast a shadow over the school that has yet to wane. According to law professors Robert D. Bickel and Peter F. Lake,

> Modern American universities often evoke images of laureled sanctuaries where higher learning is facilitated in a unique and particularly safe environment. Yet, college education is filled with potential safety risks for students. The media now reports regularly about criminal attacks on students on campus, injuries to students on field trips and in study abroad programs, . . . and of course, Greek life incidents and alcohol problems on and off campus.[1]

A central goal of this book is to make you a better-educated consumer about what colleges and universities have to offer both your son or daughter as a student and you as a parent. Part of that goal involves exposing the hazards of which Bickel and Lake write and offering lessons in how to avoid becoming a victim of your own, your child's, or someone else's negligence. Colleges and universities owe it to parents and students—their charges for four or so years—to come clean about the way things really are on campus. At the same time, parents need to open their eyes to what it is really like on many campuses and stop bringing lawsuits against colleges for things they should have taught their "adult" children not to do in the first place. The courts are filled with many justly filed, as well as frivolous, claims against colleges and universities. In this short but rich section, my aim is to help ensure that you will not be adding to the judicial backlog in the years to come because of something your child did or had done to him or her during college.

IN LOCO PARENTIS

In the place of a parent; instead of a parent; charged with a parent's rights, duties, and responsibilities.

"In loco parentis" exists when person [sic] undertakes care and control of another in absence of such supervision by latter's natural parents and in absence of formal legal approval, and is temporary in character and is not to be likened to an adoption which is permanent.[2]

The Clery Act (Campus Security Act), discussed in detail in chapter 7, and recent legal cases such as *Knoll* v. *University of Nebraska* (1999)[3] and *Coghlan* v. *Beta Theta Pi* (Idaho, 1999),[4] are reshaping the landscape for most college attorneys and many of the country's judges. The *Knoll* case involved a freshman student who suffered serious injuries in a hazing incident that began on university property and ended in an off-campus fraternity house. In the *Coghlan* case the court considered whether a university should have prevented injury to a drunken student who was seriously injured after falling from a third-floor fire escape. Earlier, the underage student had become dangerously drunk at campus fraternity parties that university employees knew about.

With cases like *Knoll* and *Coghlan* representing new, largely uncharted territory for many colleges and the public, colleges need a better approach to dealing with aberrant student behavior that endangers students and others. One of the most articulate expressions of this transition to a new approach can be found in the Bickel and Lake book *The Rights and Responsibilities of the Modern University: Who Assumes the Risks of College Life?*[5] Although Bickel and Lake's book has a primarily legal academic focus, their writing is one of the best descriptions of the evolution of college law away from in loco parentis. Beginning in the late 1960s, college law moved into the so-called no duty era in which schools were helpless legal bystanders to student life and its dangers. Eventually, the legal specialty arrived at the current reality, which Bickel and Lake have coined the "university as facilitator." In this world, the university helps the not yet fully independent student navigate the difficult transition to adulthood and independence. Communication with parents, in such cases as student drug and alcohol violations, represents a new tactic for colleges in the fight against high-risk alcohol use by college students. In a February 2001 interview, Professor Lake explained how in the years to come colleges will increasingly use parental notification as a shield against litigation that alleges that a college acted negligently in supervising a student behaving badly.[6] Parental notification will help shift responsibility to the parent or guardian. In giving its blessing to parental notification, the U.S. Congress recognized what we all know: that parental involvement is often essential in fighting high-risk drinking and in preventing injury. Often parents are surprised to learn that their child has been involved in high-risk drinking with adverse consequences.

The law is rapidly evolving to change the *Animal House* culture on college campuses. Recent court decisions show that the court system is willing to charge colleges with responsibility for student injuries that result from alcohol use. This will translate into new and tougher college regulations regarding alcohol. Students caught up in this culture may find themselves in positions where their future academic careers are threatened—especially graduate school.[7]

Law professors Bickel and Lake take exception to those who speak of a formal return to in loco parentis, including *New York Times* correspondent Ethan Bronner. In a March 3, 1999, article, Bronner argues the following:

Three decades after American college students defiantly threw off the vestiges of curfews, dress codes, and dormitory house mothers, a revolution is under way in undergraduate life that may be quieter but no less significant. Reflecting a range of societal changes—consumerism, litigiousness, a shift in intergenerational relations and increased fears about campus drinking—colleges are offering and students are often demanding greater supervision of their lives.[8]

According to Bronner, a keen observer of the college scene, the following is emerging:

a tamer campus and an updated and subtler version of "in loco parentis," the concept that educators are stand-in parents. College administrators are struggling with the two questions that are emerging as central: Are undergraduates really adults? And should they be seen as the college's customers or more as its products?[9]

Graham B. Spanier, the president of Penn State University, knows firsthand just how real parental concerns about their college student can be. The *New York Times* article quotes President Spanier as saying, "We do not want to make them more childlike. But parents are constantly contacting us asking what is going on with their kids. They want in loco parentis. Parents say, 'Give them structure.'"[10]

The *New York Times* article also notes several important trends:

- Parents stay in much closer contact with their college-age children than did those of a generation ago (at most schools today, students have phones in their rooms and access to e-mail).
- Many parents are former students who worry that their children will repeat their college years of experimentation with illicit drug use, heavy drinking, and libertine views of sex. Many parents also have much to say about college life.
- Students increasingly want to talk to someone about their varied and perhaps difficult backgrounds. More students

than before come from homes where parents are divorced or alcoholic; and many students have eating disorders, are discovering their homosexuality, or considering for the first time really, their views about religion, race, gender, and politics.[11]

So whether they want to be or not, because of litigation, media scrutiny, and growing parental concern, many colleges have found themselves taking on a kind of parental involvement. In January 2000, Princeton University's president, Harold Shapiro, ended a twenty-five-year tradition known as the sophomore ritual, or the nude Olympics, declaring that drinking associated with the event posed risks "that we can no longer tolerate." Also in 2000, Dartmouth College announced that it was ending single-sex fraternities (on which the 1978 movie *Animal House* was based). Dartmouth plans to invest tens of millions of dollars to create a new form of undergraduate experience that it hopes will better reflect, and reflect upon, its academic mission.

Many colleges are extending their freshman orientation programs to semester-long programs focused on changing the perception of college life as a seamless string of alcohol-soaked rituals at dirty fraternity houses. The best of these programs emphasize faculty and peer mentoring by older students of first-year students. The University of Wisconsin–Madison has created learning communities complete with faculty fellows based in part on Harvard's house model and Yale's college model. A separate program for parents has been created as well.

RISK MANAGEMENT

Risk management? What is that? Many colleges, particularly the smart ones, have created the position of risk manager, a staff person whose entire professional purpose is helping the university identify risks and dangers facing the college, its students, and staff. The cynical view of these individuals is of someone merely out to protect the college from litigation. While this is indeed part of their role, a good risk manager, who commands the ear of the president and chancellor, can help make the college a safer and better place for students.

Larger schools like the University of Wisconsin have created helpful Web pages that offer staff, students, and college parents indispensable information on campus risks. Wisconsin's Web page is designed to answer questions students may have about health insurance, accidents, liability, and automobiles.

In reviewing a college's risk management materials, parents and students should pay careful attention to the tone of the material. Readers should ask themselves: Is the college simply limiting its liability or is it providing students with useful information aimed at helping them lead safer lives?

The University of Wisconsin's Web page explains that the university does not provide blanket medical coverage to students or other visitors to the campus. Should injury or property damage occur as the result of the negligence of a university employee, a claim can be filed against the university. Students who have suffered financial loss because of such an incident are encouraged to contact the university's risk management office. I would advise students to first contact their parents who might also want to contact an attorney.

Work-study students, as university student employees (at least at state universities), may be covered by a state's liability protection coverage where the student's work-related negligent acts may have caused injury or property damage to others.

NINE

Your Head and What's Ahead

◨ ◨ ◨

TAKING CARE OF YOURSELF AND THE OTHERS
LEFT AT HOME

What changes at home should parents anticipate when their son or daughter leaves for college? What would I do if my son or daughter were leaving for college? While questions relating to how to pay for college and how to help a son or daughter find the right school are unquestionably important, so are your concerns about how you will feel once your child leaves home. Although so many families go through the transition of watching a child go off to college, relatively little has been written about the psychological impact of this event on the parents.

According to Dr. Elizabeth Marks, a psychiatrist in Newton, Massachusetts, a child leaving for college often serves as a watershed event in the lives of the parents, sometimes underscoring the absence of anything else in a relationship between the parents. Dr. Marks also describes the common experience many parents share in having to "bite their lip practically until it bleeds" rather than tell a son or daughter how to lead his or her life after leaving home for college.[1]

Barbara Rosen, Ph.D., a psychologist in La Jolla, California, notes that for parents, a child's departure is "not going to be anything like you think." Dr. Rosen recalls her separation from her twin sons when they left southern California for colleges across the country in New England. "I felt so prepared for their departure that I sold their car and disconnected their phone—only to end up paying the extra costs of replacements when I realized six months later that they were far from gone."[2] Dr. Rosen's experience is not at all unique in her community—a well-to-do town in which most teenagers and young adults have it pretty good, enjoy strong friendships, and are generally well treated at home. According to Dr. Rosen, it was not until a few years after college that she experienced a significant change in the nature of the relationship with her children. She adds, however, that her children might view things differently.[3]

Obviously, there is a great deal of variety in how each individual and family experiences the transition of a child leaving for college. In her practice, however, Dr. Rosen has found a general tendency among young people to deny feelings of vulnerability:

> Adolescence is generally not a time to ponder one's vulnerability but to disprove it. Most college-age young men and women are not conscious of their anxiety, burying it in one form of action or another. I think we need to see this as somewhat adaptive in most cases as well as a problem—in other words, it works for most kids and is part of our internal programming that permits us to be brave enough to strike out on our own and separate.[4]

Parents, on the other hand, are often primed to confront their mortality, the passing of time, and the existential meaning of life. Nevertheless, a child leaving for college may be a burdensome time for many—with lots of bills and few concrete payoffs—rather than the golden years of relaxation many had long anticipated. In confronting both the financial and emotional costs of sending a child off to college, it is important to recognize that you are not alone. College Parents of America, a national nonprofit advocacy group, notes that there are over 32 million U.S. households with parents of current and future college students.[5]

For families experiencing the departure of an oldest child for college, Dr. Rosen stresses the importance of giving attention to siblings during this difficult transitional time and emphasizes the importance generally of thinking about the ones left behind:

> I find in my practice that these are often the most deeply affected and ignored family members—either missing the absentee collegiate or feeling disruption in the fabric of family life as parents feel less homebound, or some combination of both.[6]

HOW WE LOOK TO THEM (LOOK WHO'S BACK)

For a different and perhaps fresh perspective on how our college-age children view us—their parents—try looking at some of the publications written for college students. In "The Parent Trap," a 2000 article from the on-line site Student.Com, University of Massachusetts social psychologist Michael Berg describes how spending a summer at home with your parents can be enough to drive anyone "nuts." When you stop giggling about the sort of advice he offers, you may find some of what he says helpful.

Berg's observations describe the first month home after freshman year in college (and might just as well describe the summer before a child leaves home for college). Berg says the following (tongue in cheek, I hope):

> Your parents will see you returning to their nest for the summer and they'll plan to protect you and nurture you just like they did for your first 18 years. They do not mean to squash your newfound independence; they are just doing what they know. Help them out. . . . Always tell them where you are going and when you will be home. . . . Meanwhile, return home each night before your estimated time of arrival. Your parents will see what a great job they did raising you and they'll stop worrying so much.[7]

In Cornell University's *Parents Guide,* the "What's Ahead?" section reads, in part, as follows:

Your relationship with your son or daughter will undergo many changes during the college years. Particularly during the first year of college, many students teeter back and forth between a continuing need to rely on parents and a desire for a new independence. Although confusing and frustrating for parents and students alike, this is a very normal part of the process of separation that will continue throughout young adulthood. You are likely to experience an adjustment every time your son or daughter comes home and every time he or she leaves again.[8]

Pat McCoy, a counselor at New Mexico State University, wrote a thoughtful essay on the changes parents and children may experience when a child leaves for college for a special summer edition of the campus newspaper. McCoy's essay is reproduced on the following pages with her permission and permission from New Mexico State University.[9]

PARENT-CHILD TRANSITION

By: Pat McCoy, Counselor
The Counseling Center
New Mexico State University
June 13, 1997

My first child will be leaving for college soon, and I have mixed feelings about this. I know things will change, yet I'm uncertain about how the changes will affect us and our relationship.

For most parents, the end of their child's required education and preparation for their child's departure marks a significant turning point for each of them and for their relationship. Because of the inevitable changes and uncertainties involved in any major life transition, both parent and child struggle with the desire to let go and the longing to hold on.

Change is not only inevitable, it is necessary for growth. Your child's entry into college is an event and a time that you have both dreamed about and dreaded, a time to move forward and a time to say farewell, a period of excitement and pride coupled with anxiety and sadness.

Not all students handle the demands of college in the same way or with equal success. Some are ready for the challenge; others require considerable support. There are the expected worries: Is he self-disciplined enough to manage his studies? Is she experienced enough to choose trustworthy dating partners? Can he resist the temptation to party too often? Will she be homesick and lonely? When to hold on and when to let go becomes an important consideration.

Hold on to the values that you have taught your child by your words and your example. Let go of the expectation that your child will hold fast to those values without wavering or questioning. College challenges students to examine their values and to make their own decisions. Hold on to trust that much of what you have taught will ultimately be incorporated into your child's personal morals and value system.

Hold on to the expectations you have about your contributions to your child's education and communicate those expectations clearly to your child. Let go of mandating what he or she will or will not do; those choices are the child's responsibility. The determination of consequences for those choices is yours to decide or to negotiate with your child.

Let go of the need to save your child from mistakes. Mistakes are a natural part of learning and call for understanding and change rather than chastisement and rejection. Hold on to support for your child's acceptance of responsibility and demonstration of improved decision-making.

Hold on to regular, open communication with your child, even if he or she pulls back for a while, distracted by the challenges of college life or determined to establish a sense of independence. Communication is even more important during this period of transition, a link with your shared past and a path for your future relationship.

Let go of the wish to maintain familiar roles and ground rules; these are bound to change as your child establishes his or her own identity and begins to assume increasing responsibility for his or her life. Hold on to the memories and the love you have for your child. These will carry you through this period of change and uncertainty, moving you toward a new, and more rewarding, adult-to-adult relationship.

College is a bridge between adolescence and adulthood. Be patient as you cross this bridge together, persevere when the crossing roughens, respect one another's visions, and learn from each other throughout the journey. The final destination is well worth the trip!

TEN

Resources for Parents

◼ ◼ ◼

GENERAL GUIDEBOOKS

Let's face it. As much as you have loved my book and found it indispensable, to help with the college search you may also want to buy one of those telephone-book-sized college directories that doubles as a booster seat at family get-togethers. That puts me in a tough spot. Under the best of circumstances, recommending a guidebook or college directory for college-bound students is no easy matter. To make matters worse, I am now the author of one. So I need a way out and I think I have found one. A June 2, 2000, article in the *Chronicle of Higher Education* describes how several of the country's leading guidebooks charge colleges to include their write-ups in the book. What started as a *Chronicle* investigative report on the book *Making a Difference College and Graduate Guide* by Miriam H. Weinstein, soon turned into an informative exposé on the guidebook industry. The *Chronicle* found that in creating her guidebook, Weinstein had neglected to note that she had accepted hundreds of dollars from colleges to be included in the book. More surprising, however, the *Chronicle* found the following:

> Other guidebooks, too, fail to disclose that many colleges essentially buy coverage. Several publishers of college directories—including Peterson's and Princeton Review, two of the largest—sell space in their books to admissions offices that want to add their own messages to the standard profiles.[1]

173

Critics cited in the *Chronicle* article call such tactics highly mis-
leading to students and parents.

"Families assume that these guidebooks are an objective source
of information, and they do not necessarily have the sophisti-
cation to realize that much of what they're reading is actually
paid advertising," says Kristin R. Tichenor, director of admissions at Clark University, in Worcester, Massachusetts.

"The reality is that families are swallowing the information
whole, without realizing that a four-page spread on a particular college may have nothing to do with the quality of the institution. It may just have to do with how much the college is
willing to spend to have their programs highlighted in a particular guidebook."[2]

Well, first let me say that I have not taken money from anyone to
put his or her work or college in a favorable light in this book. Okay,
now that that is clear, what follows is information on several guidebooks that parents and students *may* want to consider when applying
to college. After all, given the bill you will be footing for college,
what is another $15 to $20 dollars, however suspect the recommendations? Please note that much of what I have said about the guides
is based on the *Chronicle*'s coverage as well as my own impressions of
the books. In no way should inclusion of a guide herein be construed
as an endorsement of the guide. As for the ones I have described
briefly below, caveat emptor—you are on your own.

Most bookstores carry at least several of the guidebooks listed
below. Typically, the guidebooks contain information on average SAT
scores, loose rankings such as "competitive," tuition costs, student-
to-faculty ratio, and descriptions of the social life at the school.

The Insider's Guide to the Colleges, 2000
By: The Yale Daily News

I found this guidebook a comprehensive look at the colleges, with
thoughtful, generally well-written sections on the full range of issues new
students will face at college. That said, one reviewer on Amazon.com wrote
of the *Insider's Guide*, "If you are looking for more than a description of the social life at colleges, you won't get it here. All of the other info is widely avail-

able on the Internet and is much the same as in other guides. This is not a place to find any analysis of courses and programs." Another reviewer countered, "This book shows what really counts, how students see colleges. Beats the corporate propaganda books any day since it includes perspectives from actual students. A great buy."

The Fiske Guide to Getting into the Right College: The Complete Guide to Everything You Need to Know to Get into and Pay for College
By: Edward B. Fiske and Bruce G. Hammond

This guide offers a listing of the authors' pick of the three hundred "best and most interesting colleges and universities." Fiske is a former education editor at the *New York Times* and his journalistic essays often offer students and parents an entertaining read on the different schools he has chosen to feature. My personal favorite tidbit: the best place to eat at the University of Colorado, Boulder—the Packer Grill—named after a man convicted of cannibalism in 1883. The guidebook's "best buys" and "news you can use" sections are quite well written and informative.

The Princeton Review Complete Book of Colleges
Web: www.review.com

The *Complete* guide contains both standard full-page profiles of 1,500 four-year institutions as well as two-page write-ups for which some 300 schools have paid a fee. The schools that have paid for write-ups ($3,500 according to the *Chronicle*) tend to be smaller, less well-known colleges and universities. These write-ups are advertorial-like detailed descriptions of the college.

According to the June 2, 2000, article in the *Chronicle of Higher Education*, the Princeton Review,

> [also markets] its test-preparation services to students as a way for them to gain the upper hand against colleges and the producers of standardized tests. [The Review] also publishes *The Best 331 Colleges*, which may be best known for its unconventional rankings, including top "party school."[3]

Peterson's
Web: www.petersons.com

Peterson's College and University Almanac is a directory of 1,700 four-year and two-year colleges and universities. According to the *Chronicle*, "150 colleges paid for inclusion in an additional 'open forum' section of full-page descriptions." The company's Web site details that each page-long description in the "open forum" section costs $985.

Other Peterson's products include *Peterson's Four-Year Colleges* and *Competitive Colleges,* which contains fact-based profiles on about 400 institutions that routinely admit high-achieving students.

Peterson's CollegeQuest
Web: www.collegequest.com

This Web site offers students a personal organizer, practice SAT and ACT tests, and chat or discussion groups.

U.S. News and World Report's *America's Best Colleges*
Web: www.usnews.com/usnews/edu/home.htm

In addition to its guidebook available in most bookstores, U.S. News and World Report has created an on-line guide to finding the best colleges.

PUBLICATIONS ON SPECIFIC TOPICS

Campus Mental Health Issues: Best Practices—*A Guide for Colleges*

This 2000 publication is written by Meg Muckenhoupt, a Boston-area author and mental health professional. Muckenhoupt's thoughtful monograph describes the challenges that student mental health issues pose to colleges and universities. It also describes model mental health practices being used at some schools and offers advice to parents, student-affairs and residence-life staff, faculty, police, and fellow students on assisting a student who may be suffering from a mental health problem.

Copies of Muckenhoupt's publication are available from:

Attn: Campus Mental Health Issues
Health and Human Development Programs
Education Development Center, Inc.
55 Chapel Street
Newton, MA 02458-1060
Phone: (617) 618-2287
Fax: (617) 527-4096
E-mail: hhdmail@edc.org
Web: www.edc.org/hhd

A Few Words for Parents About Alcohol and College
The Michigan Department of Community Health
Bureau of Substance Abuse Services
Lewis Cass Building, Sixth Floor
320 South Walnut Street
Lansing, MI 48913
Phone: (517) 335-0278
Web: www.mdch.state.mi.us/ads/binge.htm

This booklet, produced by the Michigan Department of Community Health (MDCH), is about high-risk college student drinking. MDCH's Web site contains additional information on the topic that may be of interest to parents and college-bound students.

Alcohol, Drugs, and Your College Student
Syracuse University
Division of Student Affairs
306 Steele Hall
Syracuse, NY 13244
Phone: (315) 443-4263
Web: http://students.syr.edu

This is one of the better publications for college parents on the subject of student drug use. According to an introductory letter from the vice president and dean, the brochure is designed to help students and parents prepare for a dialogue about the dangers of alcohol and other drug abuse. The brochure emphasizes that the conversation between parents and students should be ongoing rather than a one-time talk. Syracuse, like a growing number of colleges and universities, views parents as "partners" in the challenge to combat high-risk student drinking and other drug use. The university's parental notification policy is also described.

How to Talk to Your College Age Child/Student about Alcohol and Other Drugs
Syracuse University Health Center
111 Waverly Avenue
Syracuse, NY 13244
Phone: (315) 443-4234
Web: http://sumweb.syr.edu/health/parents.htm

This is another useful publication from Syracuse University. It is produced by the Syracuse University Substance Abuse Prevention and Health Enhancement Office.

Parents, You're Not Done Yet

The Century Council
1310 G Street NW, Suite 600
Washington, DC 20005
Phone: (202) 637-0077
Fax: (202) 637-0079
Web: www.thecenturycouncil.org

This flyer, created by the Century Council, an alcohol-industry-sponsored group, enumerates things parents can tell their sons or daughters *right now,* before the students leave for college, and *once they're at college.* Because the deep-pocketed Century Council is able to print tens of thousands of copies of the brochure, many colleges send copies to parents of new students. The alcohol industry in the guise of the Century Council has also underwritten the cost of development and widespread dissemination of *Alcohol 101,* an interactive CD-ROM for students, which is designed to better inform users of the risks of high-risk drinking. As parents of college-bound students, you may have already received a copy of the brochure. Once your son or daughter starts school, he or she may be exposed to the *Alcohol 101* CD-ROM. Recognizing the need—that colleges and universities were starved for attractively designed and *free-of-charge* prevention materials—the Century Council has done an excellent job of widely disseminating its materials.

College Newspapers

Web: www.uwire.com

Reading the college newspapers is a good way to learn what is occuring on campus and to discover more about the campus and college culture. While many college papers have their own easy-to-find Web sites, CPNet and UWIRE permit you to read news from college newspapers across the country.

ORGANIZATIONS AND FOUNDATIONS

The Campus Safety Website

The U.S. Department of Education's Office of Postsecondary Education
Web: http://ope.ed.gov/security

This congressionally authorized Web site is supposed to feature campus crime statistics for all of the nation's 6,000-plus colleges and universities. While I welcomed the fall 2000 opening of the site and urge parents and students to make use of it, I have many doubts about the accuracy of many colleges' self-reports of campus crime. Chapter 7, "Safe and Sound," contains a detailed discussion of campus safety issues and compliance by colleges with the reporting requirements of the Clery Act.

The College Board

Web: www.collegeboard.com

This extensive Web site contains on-line registration for the SAT as well as advice on writing college application essays. As of this printing, the College Board was planning to launch a Web feature called "LikeFinder" that will help students identify colleges similar to the ones they are already researching. Another planned Web feature will offer students side-by-side comparisons of selected colleges.

CollegeLink

Web: www.collegelink.com

This college financial aid site offers a month-by-month financial planner and informative articles about college financial aid.

College Parents of America

700 13th Street NW, Suite 950
Washington, DC 20005
Phone: (888) 256-4627, (202) 661-2170
Web: www.collegeparents.org

College Parents of America (CPA) is a national membership organization that provides a voice for parents of current and prospective college students. The group provides information to parents and also represents the needs of these parents at congressional hearings, at higher education symposiums, and in state legislatures. CPA focuses on alcohol and drug problems on campus, among other issues, and offers a newsletter and a variety of member discounts on a range of products and services.

CPA is a national membership association dedicated to helping parents prepare and put their children through college easily, economically, and safely. Today, college parents represent an estimated twelve million households. An additional twenty-four million households are currently saving and otherwise preparing children for college. CPA is a resource, an advisor, and an advocate working on behalf of these families.

Combating Alcohol Abuse on Campus—CPA launched this initiative in the fall of 1997 with the U.S. Department of Education's Higher Education Center for Alcohol and Other Drug Prevention to combat alcohol abuse on campus. CPA is working to advise parents on how to talk with their children about the impact of high-risk drinking on their lives as well as their responsibilities to their peers. Negotiations may also lead to reduced insurance premiums for students signing pledges. In addition, CPA and the center are promoting further involvement of parents and other parties to help combat alcohol abuse.

Fastweb
Web: www.fastweb.com
   Fastweb is an on-line database of grants and student scholarships. The site is another you want to be sure to bookmark for your son or daughter.

FAFSA (Federal Student Aid)
Web: www.fafsa.ed.gov
   This Web site offers an on-line version of the federal financial aid form. Chapter 2, "Paying for College and Getting What You Pay For" contains a detailed discussion of FAFSA.

FINAID: The SmartStudent Guide to Financial Aid
Web: www.finaid.org
   This useful Web site features on-line calculators and resources for parents and students on college financial aid.

Handling Your Psychiatric Disability in Work and School
Web: www.bu.edu/sarpsych/jobschool
Center for Psychiatric Rehabilitation
Sargent College of Health and Rehabilitation Sciences
Boston University
940 Commonwealth Avenue West
Boston, MA 02215
Phone: (617) 353-3549
Fax: (617) 353-7700
TTY: (617) 353-7701
   Boston University's Center for Psychiatric Rehabilitation has created this informative interactive Web site for people with psychiatric disabilities. The

Web site addresses issues related to work and school and includes information about the Americans with Disabilities Act (ADA).

Short informative features available on the Web site include the following:

- How does mental illness affect the way a mentally disabled person functions at school?
- Basic study skills for students
- Academic adjustment issues in the classroom
- Documenting your disability for an educational institution
- How to make decisions about one's education as a psychiatrically disabled person.

The Web site also contains useful links to school-related sites and maintains a listing of those who would like to be contacted via e-mail about announcements and special events at the Center.

Hazelden

P.O. Box 11, CO 3
Center City, MN 55012-0011
Phone: (800) 257-7810 (bookstore information)
Web: www.hazelden.org

The Hazelden Foundation is a nonprofit organization providing rehabilitation, education, prevention, and professional services in chemical dependency and related disorders.

Hazelden is also the publisher of a number of useful books, curricula, pamphlets, videos, and trainings on a wide range of parenting topics, from basic skills to how to talk to kids about alcohol and drugs and how to intervene on use.

The Higher Education Center for Alcohol and Other Drug Prevention

Health and Human Development Programs
Education Development Center, Inc.
55 Chapel Street
Newton, MA 02458-1060
Phone: (800) 676-1730
Fax: (617) 928-1537
E-mail: HigherEdCtr@edc.org
Web: www.edc.org/hec

The Higher Education Center is the nation's leading provider of training and technical assistance to colleges and universities seeking to develop, implement, and evaluate effective programs and policies for the prevention of high-risk drinking and other drug use. The center, established by the U.S. Department of Education in 1993, has been operated since 1995 by a team of professionals based at Health and Human Development Programs (www.edc.org/hhd), a division of Education Development Center, Inc. (EDC), in Newton, Massachusetts. Health and Human Development Programs operates the center in partnership with the Boston University School of Public Health; the University of California–San Diego; and Social and Health Services.

Under Health and Human Development Program's management, the center has focused on improving campus policy and on the development and support of state and local prevention initiatives.

Practice has shown that the best substance-abuse and violence-prevention programs are campus-wide efforts that involve as many parts of the college as possible, including top administrators, students, staff, and faculty. Building coalitions with local community leaders and treatment resources is also key. Prevention planners need to collaborate with local leaders to limit student access to alcohol and other drugs, support referral to treatment, and support the efforts of local law enforcement.

Alcohol, Other Drugs, and College: A Parent's Guide

In 2000, the Higher Education Center published *Alcohol, Other Drugs, and College: A Parent's Guide,* offering tips to parents on what to look for and ask about when visiting college campuses. The Higher Education Center has distributed this valuable resource to high school guidance counselors at more than thirty thousand schools around the country so that counselors can pass this information on to concerned parents and prospective students.

In 2000, the Higher Education Center also published descriptions of prevention programs that have addressed the substance abuse problem on their campuses with some success. *Alcohol and Other Drug Prevention on College Campuses: Model Programs 1999 and 2000* outlines the programs at thirteen colleges and universities chosen by the U.S. Department of Education for their innovative alcohol or other drug prevention programs. According to the Higher Education Center, the descriptions of these model programs can further inform concerned parents and students in search of a safe campus.

National Association for College Admission Counseling (NACAC)
1631 Prince Street
Alexandria, VA 22314-2818
Phone: (703) 836-2222
Fax: (703) 836-8015
Fax-on-demand: (703) 299-6829
Web: www.nacac.com

NACAC is an education association of more than 6,900 secondary school guidance counselors, college admission officers, financial aid officers, and independent counselors who work with students as they make the transition from high school to postsecondary education. According to NACAC, college admission counselors are often the primary sources of information about the transition process and are uniquely aware of the concerns held by the people they serve.

To help college-bound students and their parents interact one-on-one with college admission representatives from around the United States, NACAC has created *Online College Fair*, a free program designed to help students and parents navigate the college search, admissions, and financial aid processes. During these on-line, interactive fairs, students and parents can log on to www.OnlineCollegeFair.com to chat live with representatives from more than one hundred colleges and universities, view college campuses, and learn what each institution has to offer in a virtual Q&A. Students can also join live sessions on topics such as financial aid and scholarships, test preparation, and college counseling that are moderated by admission community experts. Each participating institution hosts its own multimedia chat room. Admissions staff, faculty, and current students staff the chat rooms. The NACAC Web site also lists a schedule of upcoming Online College Fairs and additional information, including the list of participating colleges. In 2000, more than 400,000 students and their families explored their options for higher education at a NACAC college fair.

National Center for Education Statistics/
IPEDS College Opportunities
Web: www.nces.ed.gov/ipeds/cool

Bookmark this Web site for your college-bound son or daughter. It features a searchable database of nine thousand colleges. Students can conduct customized searches for colleges that meet the criteria that they set forth.

The National Center for Public Policy and Higher Education
Web: www.highereducation.org
San Jose Office
152 North Third Street, Suite 705
San Jose, CA 95112
Phone: (408) 271-2699
Fax: (408) 271-2697
E-mail: center@highereducation.org
Washington, D.C., Office
1001 Connecticut Avenue NW, Suite 310
Washington, DC 20036
Phone: (202) 822-6720
Fax: (202) 822-6730

The National Center for Public Policy and Higher Education works to strengthen America's future by increasing opportunity and achievement for all who aspire to higher education. As an independent, nonprofit, nonpartisan organization, the center promotes public policies that enhance Americans' opportunities to pursue and achieve high-quality education and training beyond high school. Established in 1998, the National Center for Public Policy and Higher Education is not associated with any institution of higher education, with any political party, or with any government agency; it is supported by a consortium of national foundations that includes the Pew Charitable Trusts and the Ford Foundation.

In November 2000, the National Center for Public Policy and Higher Education released *Measuring Up 2000,* the first report card measuring state performance in higher education. The report grades states using "A" through "F" grades in five key areas of higher education performance: preparation, participation, affordability, completion, and benefits.

The National Resource Center for the First-Year Experience and Students in Transition
1629 Pendleton Street
University of South Carolina
Columbia, SC 29208
Phone: (803) 777-6029
Fax: (803) 777-4699
E-mail: fyeconf@gwm.sc.edu
Web: www.sc.edu/fye

The National Resource Center for the First-Year Experience and Students in Transition at the University of South Carolina, chartered in 1986, is an outgrowth and extension of the University 101 first-year seminar course begun at USC in 1972. The center collects and disseminates information about the first college year and other significant student transitions. This information is used to help educators enhance the learning, success, satisfaction, and retention of college students in transition.

Phoenix House Children of Alcoholics Foundation
164 West 74th Street
New York, NY 10023
Phone: (212) 595-5810, ext. 7760
Fax: (212) 595-2553
Web: www.coaf.org

Founded in 1982, the Phoenix House Children of Alcoholics Foundation (COAF) is a nonprofit organization dedicated to breaking the cycle of family substance abuse. COAF provides materials, curricula, and training for a range of audiences including children (COAs) and adults (ACOAs) from alcoholic and substance-abusing families, as well as professionals who work with these individuals. Among COAF's many programs are "Facts on Tap," with a component for college students who are ACOAs; "The Ties That Bind," for kinship caregivers; "Discovering Normal," for parents who are ACOAs; and "Opening and Closing Pandora's Box," for medical professionals on how to discuss sensitive topics.

SAFETI Clearinghouse
Center for Global Education
Rossier School of Education, WPH-904D
University of Southern California
Los Angeles, CA 90089-0031
Phone: (213) 740-7933
Fax: (213) 740-0439
E-mail: rhodes@usc.edu
Web: www.usc.edu/globaled/safeti

The SAFETI (Safety Abroad First—Educational Travel Information) Clearinghouse Project at the University of Southern California is a health and safety information resource center for study abroad programs. While mostly a Web site for foreign study program administrators, from time to time, the SAFETI on-line newsletter features articles that will be of interest to parents of college students.

Security on Campus, Inc.

601 South Henderson Road, Suite 205
King of Prussia, PA 19406-3596
Phone: (888) 251-7959, (610) 768-9330
Fax: (610) 768-0646
Web: http://campussafety.org

Security on Campus is a nonprofit organization dedicated to crime prevention on college campuses. The group's extensive Web site contains important information about campus crime and what can be done to prevent it. Security on Campus and Howard and Connie Clery, the group's founders, have been critical in the movement to improve campus crime reporting by colleges and universities. The federal campus crime reporting law—the Jeanne Clery Act—is named in memory of the Clerys' daughter, who was killed by a fellow student at Lehigh University in the late 1980s.

Solutions

P.O. Box 630337
Little Neck, NY 11363-0337
Phone: (516) 466-8083
E-mail: dfz@prodigy.net

Solutions is a New York–based firm of professional organizers with a focus on parents and children. Diana Zimmerman, the company's president, is a frequent lecturer and the author of a series of helpful brochures for parents and students. The "How Am I Supposed to Know That?" series includes the brochures "The Ultimate College Checklist" and "Your First Apartment." Other areas in which Solutions has developed training and informational material include keeping in touch with a child away at college and packing the car for that first trip to college.

StopHazing.org

Web: www.stophazing.org

This Web site offers a wealth of information on hazing, with a list of relevant books. Hank Nuwer's *Wrongs of Passage* (Indiana University Press, 1999) is among the books featured.

98six

Web: www.98six.com

This relatively new Web site bills itself as one that parents and students may want to visit with questions about student heath concerns. The site, launched in January 2000 by Rethink Inc., calls itself a national college health Web site for students. It provides health-related content.

The Author As an Ongoing Resource

That is about it. Please know that your voices and concerns are being heard. College life is getting more and more parent-friendly by the day. Just remember, colleges need you and your child far more than the tuition they have the chutzpah to charge suggests.

Many people helped me to identify and develop the material that is presented in this book. None, however, were more important than the many college parents who offered their critical perspectives on the challenges they faced in sending a son or daughter off to college. Please keep in touch by sharing your experiences, anecdotes, criticism, and suggestions for making future editions of this book even better. My address is: Joel Epstein, c/o Hazelden Publishing and Educational Services, P.O. Box 176, Center City, MN 55012-0176, and my e-mail address is: jepstein@hazelden.org.

Notes

INTRODUCTION

1. Dr. Tim Brooks, interview with author, 22 June 2000.
2. Jon Kirshner, interview with author, 4 November 2000.
3. John Gardner, interview with author, 16 October 2000.
4. "Q & A with John Gardner," *Prevention File* 15, no. 2 (spring 2000). Available on-line: <www.edc.org/hec/pubs/articles/prevfile0004.html> (accessed 22 April 2001).

CHAPTER 1: THE RIGHT SCHOOL FOR YOUR CHILD — AND YOU

1. National Center for Education Statistics. See <http://nces.ed.gov> (accessed 21 February 2001).
2. Christopher J. Lucas, *American Higher Education: A History* (New York: St. Martin's Press, 1994).
3. National Center for Education Statistics.
4. Steven M. Ward, interview with author, 28 April 2000. Chief Ward is a frequent lecturer on trends in American higher education.
5. Educational Testing Service. See <www.ets.org> (accessed 21 February 2001).
6. Ibid.
7. Lauren (last name withheld), interview with author, 28 June 2000.
8. Ibid.
9. Core Institute, Southern Illinois University, Carbondale, Ill. See <www.siu.edu/departments/coreinst/public_html> (accessed 21 February 2001); National Institute on Alcohol Abuse and Alcoholism

(NIAAA), Rockville, Md. See <www.niaaa.nih.gov/about/college/ default.htm> (accessed 21 February 2001).

10. Jacques Steinberg, "Role Reversal Time for College Supplicants," *New York Times,* 3 May 2000.

11. College Night, Demarest, N.J., Fall 2000.

12. "Questions to Ask on a Campus Visit," *U.S. News and World Report: Annual College Issue* (2000). Available on-line: <www.usnews.com/ usnews/edu/college/articles/2_6_2.htm> (accessed 22 April 2001).

13. Reprinted with permission from the National Association for College Admission Counseling (NACAC). NACAC's Web site contains additional material that may be of interest to students (and parents) selecting a college. See <www.nacac.com>.

14. Campus tour guides at Harvard University and Boston College, interviews with author, fall 2000.

15. See Dan Carnevale, "Colleges Experiment with Videoconferencing to Answer Questions of Potential Applicants," *Chronicle of Higher Education,* 5 May 2000.

16. Belle Frank, interview with author, 22 January 2001.

17. Steinberg, "Role Reversal Time for College Supplicants."

18. Frank, interview with author.

19. Karen Zweig, interview with author, 2 October 2000.

20. Mark Blaudschun, "A Hot Topic at Dinner Table," *Boston Globe,* 21 June 2000.

21. James C. McKinley Jr., "Decision on Knight Shows the Fine Line That Colleges Walk," *New York Times,* 21 May 2000. For more about college athletics, see Murray Sperber, *Beer and Circus: How Big-Time College Sports Is Crippling Undergraduate Education* (New York: Henry Holt and Company, 2000).

22. McKinley, "Decision on Knight."

23. Andrea Vogt, "WSU Tries to Polish Its Image—University Claims Recent Student Mayhem, Fishbowl Setting Conspire to Eclipse Good Side," *Spokane.net,* 16 April 2000.

24. Peter F. Lake, interview with author, 6 February 2001.

25. Judith Rodin, "The University and a Civil Society," paper presented at Chubb Fellow Lecture, Yale University, 12 October 1999). Available online: <www.upenn.edu/almanac/v46/n12/rodin2yale.html> (accessed 22 April 2001).

26. Jodi Wilgoren, "At One University, Public Service Is Given a School of Its Own," *New York Times,* 21 April 2000.

27. Ibid.

28. For more information about Campus Compact, see <www.compact.org>.

29. Vision Statement, last updated 9 March 1999, Tufts University. Available on-line: <www.tufts.edu/ir/vision.html> (accessed 22 April 2001).

30. *Colleges That Encourage Character Development: A Resource for Parents, Students, and Educators (The Templeton Guide)* (Philadelphia: John Templeton Foundation, 1999).

31. Dan Carnevale, "New U. of California Campus Is Taking Classes to Its Students," *Chronicle of Higher Education,* 19 April 2000.

32. Ibid.

33. Ibid.

34. Matthew S. Santirocco, interview with author, 23 January 2001.

35. Kelly Nelson, "Advice for Transfer Students," *U.S. News and World Report,* 22 April 2000. Available on-line: <www.usnews.com/usnews/edu/college/articles/cotrans.htm> (accessed 22 April 2001).

36. For a discussion of the role parents and others can play in helping a student suffering from depression, see Meg Muckenhoupt, *Campus Mental Health Issues: Best Practices—A Guide for Colleges* (Newton, Mass.: Health and Human Development Programs, Education Development Center, 2000); <www.edc.org/HHD>.

37. Dr. Seuss, *Oh, the Places You'll Go* (New York: Random House, 1990).

38. *Oh, the Places You'll Go,* Library of Congress Cataloging-in-Publication summary, p. 1.

CHAPTER 2: PAYING FOR COLLEGE AND GETTING WHAT YOU PAY FOR

1. Diane Schulman, interview with author, 27 May 1998.

2. National Center for Education Statistics. See <www.nces.ed.gov>.

3. Miles A. Rubin, interview with author, 31 January 2001.

4. Ibid.

5. Ibid.

6. Jeffrey M. Sherman, interview with author, 4 February 2001.

7. Ibid.

8. Rand Hutcheson, interview with author, 15 February 2001.

9. David Braze, "Qualified State Tuition Plans," *The Motley Fool,* 22 January 2001. Available on-line: <www.fool.com/retirement/retirereport/2001/retirereport010122.htm> (accessed 22 April 2001). As of this writing, only Georgia and South Dakota had no plans, although Georgia was close to enacting a program.

10. Hutcheson, interview with author.
11. Ibid.
12. See Internal Revenue Code, section 135.
13. Hutcheson, interview with author.
14. Deborah Hahn, interview with author, 18 May 2000.
15. See <www.umich.edu>.
16. William DeJong, interview with author, 30 January 2001.
17. See <www.umich.edu>.
18. Gordon M. Henry, interview with author, 6 February 2001.
19. See Robert D. Manning, *Credit Card Nation: The Consequences of America's Addiction to Credit* (New York: Basic Books, 2000).
20. *Financial Services Study* (Ridgewood, N.J.: Student Monitor, LLC: spring 2000).
21. Linda Downing, quoted in Todd Abrams, "Choose Your Cards Wisely." Available on-line: <www.student.com/article/creditcarddebt> (accessed 22 April 2001).
22. Bob Rollins, interview with author, 3 December 2000.
23. Diana Zimmerman, interview with author, 8 May 2000.

CHAPTER 3: CHOOSING A COURSE OF STUDY AND OTHER ACADEMIC CONCERNS

1. Gordon M. Henry, interview with author, 7 February 2001.
2. Burton Bollag, "Dutch Fraternities Are Booming as European Counterparts Shrink—Beer and Study Are an Irresistible Draw to the Netherlands' Fraternal Groups," *Chronicle of Higher Education*, 19 May 2000.
3. Deborah Hahn, interview with author, 25 September 2000.
4. John Katzman, interview with author, 8 February 2001.
5. Kenneth Breuer, interview with author, 8 February 2001.
6. Anne Foster, interview with author, 7 February 2001.
7. Hervey Pean, "Virtual Fake Outs—Where Have You Seen That Paper Before? Uh, Probably Online." Available on-line: <www.student.com> (accessed 21 February 2001).
8. Foster, interview with author.
9. See Joseph Gibaldi, *MLA Handbook for Writers of Research Papers,* 5th ed., (New York: Modern Language Association, 1999); see also "A Guide for Writing Research Papers," (Hartford, Conn.: Capital Community College, June 2000). Available on-line: <http://webster.commnet.edu/mla.htm> (accessed 22 April 2001).

10. William DeJong, interview with author, 7 February 2001.

CHAPTER 4: LIVING THE STUDENT LIFE

1. (Name withheld), interview with author, 23 October 2000.
2. Kit Williams, interview with author, 23 October 2000.
3. Ibid.
4. Ibid.
5. Ibid.
6. Ibid.
7. *Parents Guide* (Ithaca, N.Y.: New Students Program, Office of the Dean of Students, Cornell University, 2001). Also see *Colonial Parents' Connection* (George Washington University); *Harvard College Parents Newsletter* (Harvard University); *Parents News* (New York University); *Penn Parents* (University of Pennsylvania); *Parents Pride* (Towson University).
8. Rebecca McCarthy, "UGA Official Pushes Idea of Delayed Fraternity Rush," *Atlanta Journal-Constitution*, 13 May 2000.
9. Ibid.
10. Sue Kraft Fussell. See <www.fraternityadvisors.org> (accessed 21 February 2001).
11. *A Parent's Guide to Fraternities—How Can Your Son Benefit from Fraternity Membership?* (Indianapolis, Ind.: North-American Interfraternity Conference, 2000). See <www.nicindy.org>.
12. Ibid.
13. David Abel, "Dartmouth Curbs, But Doesn't Ban, Its Frat 'Animal Houses,'" *Boston Globe*, 21 April 2000.
14. Ibid.
15. Ibid.
16. Holly Sateia, at a meeting at Green Mountain College, Poultney, Vt., 28 June 2000.
17. U.S. Department of Education's Higher Education Center for Alcohol and Other Drug Prevention, e-mail to subscribers, spring 2000. See <www.edc.org/hec>. The center is operated by Health and Human Development Programs, a division of Education Development Center, Newton, Mass. See <www.edc.org/hhd>.
18. Hank Nuwer, *Wrongs of Passage: Fraternities, Sororities, Hazing, and Binge Drinking* (Bloomington, Ind.: Indiana University Press, 1999).
19. Karl Lindholm, at a meeting at Green Mountain College, Poultney, Vt., 28 June 2000.

20. Janelle Farris, interview with author, 22 December 2000.

21. Ibid.

22. B. Ward Fletcher and J. Epstein, "AOD Prevention at Historically Black Colleges and Universities," *Catalyst* (Newton, Mass.: Higher Education Center for Alcohol and Other Drug Prevention, Winter 1996). See <www.edc.org/hec>.

23. Farris, interview with author.

24. Barbara J. Kiviat, "Presidential Summit Focuses on Helping Disabled Youths Make Transition to College and Careers," *Chronicle of Higher Education,* 22 June 2000.

25. Ibid.

26. Samuel G. Freedman, *Jew vs. Jew* (New York: Simon and Schuster, 2000).

27. United Ministry at Harvard and Radcliffe. See <www.ministry.harvard.edu>.

28. Ibid.

29. Rabbi Benjamin Samuels, interview with author, 1 February 2001.

30. Anne Foster, interview with author, 2 January 2001.

31. Christopher T. Pierson and Lelia B. Helms, "Liquor and Lawsuits: Forty Years of Litigation Over Alcohol on Campus," *Education Law Reporter,* 11 May 2000.

32. William DeJong, interview with author, 5 January 2001. Dr. DeJong is also a professor of health communications at the Boston University School of Public Health.

33. Laura Gomberg, interview with author, 5 January 2001.

34. DeJong, interview with author.

35. Burton Bollag, "Dutch Fraternities Are Booming as European Counterparts Shrink—Beer and Study Are an Irresistible Draw to the Netherlands' Fraternal Groups," *Chronicle of Higher Education,* 19 May 2000.

36. (Name withheld), interview with author, 8 September 2000.

37. Bollag, "Dutch Fraternities Are Booming as European Counterparts Shrink."

38. Pierson and Helms, "Liquor and Lawsuits."

39. Peter F. Lake, interview with author, 6 February 2001; *The Rights and Responsibilities of the Modern University: Who Assumes the Risks of College Life?* (Durham, N.C.: Carolina Academic Press, 1999).

40. See Henry Wechsler, Toben Nelson, and Elissa Weitzman, "From Knowledge to Action: How Harvard's College Alcohol Study Can Help Your Campus Design a Campaign against Student Alcohol Abuse," *Change Magazine,* January/February 2000.

CHAPTER 5: BOTTLES, KEGS, AND OTHER VICES

1. *A Few Words for Parents about Alcohol and College* (Lansing, Mich.: Michgan Department of Community Health, 1999).
2. *Youth Risk Behavior Survey,* Centers for Disease Control and Prevention, June 2000. Available on-line: <www.cdc.gov/nccdphp/dash/yrbs> (accessed 22 April 2001).
3. Graham Spanier, Address to the National Press Club, Washington, D.C., 26 August 1999.
4. Holly Sateia, at a conference at Green Mountain College, Poultney, Vt., 28 June 2000.
5. Jeffrey Levy, interview with author, 19 May 2000.
6. Josh Slater, interview with author, 11 September 2000.
7. Levy, interview with author.
8. "New Alcohol Coordinator Gets High Marks," *Penn Parents* (University of Pennsylvania) December 1999.
9. Stephanie Ives, interview with author, 5 June 2000.
10. Harry Lewis, "On Alcohol in the College—A Message from the Dean," *Parents Newsletter* (Harvard College), Winter 2000.
11. Ibid.
12. Jane Frantz, interview with author, 30 June 2000.
13. Ibid.
14. Ibid.
15. John Gardner, interview with author, 7 November 1999.
16. "Q & A with John Gardner," *Prevention File* 15, no. 2 (Spring 2000). Available on-line: <www.edc.org/hec/pubs/articles/prevfile0004.html> (accessed 22 April 2001); Peter F. Lake, interview with author, 6 February 2001.
17. Center for Science in the Public Interest. See <www.hadenough.org>.
18. "In Their Own Words . . . Students' Stories on Alcohol and Campus Life." Available on-line: <www.cspinet.org/booze/hadenough/campuslife/studentstories.html> (accessed 22 April 2001).
19. Linda Devine and William DeJong, "What Parents Should Say to College Freshmen about Alcohol," *This Week,* 5 March 1998. Available on-line: <www.edc.org/hec/thisweek/tw980305.html> (accessed 22 April 2001).
20. William DeJong, interview with author, 5 January 2001.
21. Adam Rosen, interview with author, 15 April 2001.
22. Steve Hedrick, interview with author, 16 February 2000.
23. DeJong, interview with author.

24. Rosen, interview with author.

25. College students from Cornell University, Boston University, Harvard University, Emory University, Clemson University, and University of California–Berkeley (names withheld), interviews with author, spring 2001.

26. Carol Falkowski, *Dangerous Drugs: An Easy-to-Use Reference for Parents and Professionals* (Center City, Minn.: Hazelden, 2000), 127.

27. Adam Rosen, interview with author, 9 December 2000.

28. George Ricaurte, "Long-term Effects of 3,4-Methylenedioxymethamphetamine (MDMA, 'ecstasy') on Brain Serotonin Nerve Cells in Animals and Humans," *Addictions 1997: An International Research Journal,* 1997. Available on-line <www.vitanova.on.ca/Addictions_1997_Article_4.html> (accessed 22 April 2001).

29. Adam Rosen, interview with author, 15 April 2001.

30. Joel C. Epstein, "Parental Notification: Fact or Fiction," *Prevention File* 14, no. 2. Available on-line: <www.edc.org/hec/pubs/articles/parentalnotification.html> (accessed 22 April 2001).

31. Jessica Kirshner, interview with author, 12 March 1998.

32. Ibid.

33. (Name withheld), interview with author, 7 July 2000.

34. Jeffrey Levy and Howard Clery, interviews with author, August 2000.

35. Levy, interview with author.

36. Robert L. Barchi, interview with author, 5 June 2000.

37. DeJong, interview with author.

38. Michelle Goldfarb, interview with author, 5 June 2000.

39. Thomas King, interview with author, 5 June 2000.

40. William DeJong and Karen Zweig, "What College Catalogs Don't Tell You about Alcohol and Other Drugs on Campus," Higher Education Center for Alcohol and Other Drug Prevention, 1998. This article is no longer available on-line, but another excellent source of information for parents is the Higher Education Center's *Parent Connection.* See <www.edc.org/hec/parents>.

41. DeJong, interview with author.

42. DeJong and Zweig, "What College Catalogs Don't Tell You."

43. Ibid.

CHAPTER 6: HEALTH IS ACADEMIC

1. Jane Frantz, interview with author, 15 July 2000.

2. (Name withheld), interview with author, 2 August 2000.

3. Dan Wohlfeiler, interview with author, 18 July 2000.

4. Julia E. Rosenbaum, interview with author, 20 October 2000.

5. Sam Eifling, "Meningitis Scares at Colleges Prompt NU to Warn Students," *Daily Northwestern,* 4 May 1998. Available on-line: <www.dailynorthwestern.com/daily/issues/1998/05/04/campus/meningitis.html> (accessed 22 April 2001).

6. Centers for Disease Control and Prevention, Division of Bacterial and Mycotic Diseases, "Meningococcal Disease among College Students: ACIP Modifies Recommendations for Meningitis Vaccination," press release, 20 October 1999. Available on-line: <www.cdc.gov/ncidod/dbmc/diseaseinfo/menigococcal_college.htm> (accessed 22 April 2001).

7. Eric Rubin, interview with author, 4 February 2001.

8. Ibid.

9. American College Health Association Online, "Frequently Asked Questions (Meningococcal Meningitis)." Available on-line: <www.acha.org/special-prj/men/faq.htm> (accessed 22 April 2001).

10. Rubin, interview with author.

11. (Name withheld), interview with author, 7 December 2000.

12. Michelle Navarro, "Fight of the Freshman Fifteen: Can Students Stop the Urge to Chomp?" 1999. Available on-line:<www.student.com/article/freshmanfifteen> (accessed 22 April 2000).

13. Adam Rosen, interview with author, 3 December 2000.

14. R. C. Kessler, K. A. McGonagle, S. Zhao, C. B. Nelson, M. Hughes, S. Eshleman, H. U. Wittchen, and K. S. Kendler, "Lifetime and 12-Month Prevalence of DSM-III-R Psychiatric Disorders in the United States: Results from the National Comorbidity Survey," *Archives of General Psychiatry* 51 (1994): 413–20.

15. R. C. Kessler, quoted in Summer M. Berman, Shari Strauss, and Natasha Verhage, "Treating Mental Illness in Students: A New Strategy," *Chronicle of Higher Education,* 16 June 2000.

16. Summer M. Berman, Shari Strauss, and Natasha Verhage, "Treating Mental Illness in Students: A New Strategy," *Chronicle of Higher Education,* 16 June 2000.

17. Meg Muckenhoupt, interview with author, 2 January 2001; *Campus Mental Health Issues: Best Practices—A Guide for Colleges* (Newton, Mass.: Health and Human Development Programs, EDC, 2000), 1.

18. Sylvia H. Epstein, interview with author, 3 December 2000.

19. Berman, Strauss, and Verhage, "Treating Mental Illness in Students."

20. Muckenhoupt, interview with author.

21. Berman, Strauss, and Verhage, "Treating Mental Illness in Students."

22. Ibid.

23. Ibid.

24. Barbara Rosen, interview with author, 20 July 2000.

25. Adam Rosen, interview with author.

26. Ibid.

27. Anne Foster, interview with author, 2 January 2001.

28. Andrew E. Kuhn, interview with author, 10 July 2000.

29. Stanley Epstein, interview with author, 26 May 2000.

30. Jonathan Benjamin, interview with author, 8 April 2000.

31. Kit Williams, interview with author, 7 July 2000.

32. Ibid.

33. Benjamin, interview with author.

34. Ibid.

35. Ibid.

36. Jonathan Bertman, interview with author, 31 December 2000.

37. Benjamin, interview with author.

38. William DeJong, interview with author, 5 January 2001.

39. American College Health Association. See <www.acha.org> (accessed 21 February 2001).

40. Leo Reisberg, "Colleges Start Clinics for Doctor-Averse Men—Centers Seek to Promote Healthy Habits and to Combat Sexually Transmitted Diseases," *Chronicle of Higher Education,* 7 July 2000.

41. Ibid.

42. Peter F. Lake, interview with author, 6 February 2001.

43. Bertman, interview with author.

44. Cho Hyun, quoted in David Abel and Daryl Khan, "Anguish, But Few Answers, in MIT Suicide," *Boston Globe,* 21 May 2000.

45. Elissa Grad, interview with author, 7 May 2000.

46. Sylvia Epstein, interview with author.

CHAPTER 7: SAFE AND SOUND

1. The 2000–2001 school year was a particularly difficult one for colleges. Incidents involving four campuses in particular caught the public's attention: (1) two separate student murders at Gallaudet University in Washington, D.C., (2) the January 2001 murders of two professors at Dartmouth College in rural Hanover, New Hampshire, (3) the killing of four people and the critical injuring of a fifth by a college student who drove his car into a crowd of people near the University of California–Santa Barbara campus, and (4) the January 2001 arrest of a DeAnza College student accused of planning a "Columbine"-like attack on the Cupertino, California, campus. See David L. Marcus, "The

Campus Carnage: After a Spate of Killing a Search for Answers," *U.S. News and World Report,* 19 February 2001. Available on-line: <www.us-news.com/usnews/issue/010219/campus.htm> (accessed 22 April 2001); "Extradition for Suspect in 2 Killings at Dartmouth," *New York Times,* 21 February 2001; "Student Accused of Murdering Four Pedestrians," 27 February 2001. Available on-line: <www.msnbc.com/local/knbc/626170.asp> (accessed 22 April 2001).

2. National Center for Higher Education Risk Management (NCHERM). See <www.ncherm.org/ncherm/homepage.cfm> (accessed 22 April 2001).

3. S. Daniel Carter, interview with author, 8 June 2000.

4. Security on Campus, College and University Campus Safety Information On-line, "Campus Safety: Tips and Evaluation Brochure." Available on-line: <www.campussafety.org> (accessed 22 April 2001).

5. Cathy Kirshner, interview with author, 15 May 2000.

6. Carter, interview with author.

7. Stephen Burd, "House Votes to Require Colleges to Identify Sex Offenders," *Chronicle of Higher Education,* 23 June 2000.

8. See Michael Clay Smith and Richard Fossey, *Crime on Campus—Legal Issues and Campus Administration* (Phoenix, Ariz.: American Council on Education Series on Higher Education, Oryx Press, 1995).

9. Julie L. Nicklin, "Arrests at Colleges Surge for Alcohol and Drug Violations—Experts Cite Tougher Enforcement and a Change in Federal Law," *Chronicle of Higher Education,* 9 June 2000.

10. Leo Reisberg, "Coming to a Campus Near You: Racist Hazing with Deadly Consequences—A Real Incident Inspires an Independent Film Set at a Fictional College," *Chronicle of Higher Education,* 14 April 2000. Available on-line: <www.chronicle.com/weekly/v46/i32/32a06601.htm> (accessed 22 April 2001).

11. Joel Epstein, "Controlling Hate Crimes in the Ivory Tower," *Journal of College and Character* (Tallahassee, Fla.: Center for the Study of Values in College Student Development, Florida State University, July 2000). Available on-line: <http://collegevalues.org/ethics.cfm?id=209&a=1> (accessed 22 April 2001).

12. Ibid.

13. "Around the Nation," *10 Campus Crime 3* (Silver Spring, Md.: Business Publishers, 2000), 23.

14. Joseph S. Pete, "Transfer Screening Process Implemented after Slaying," *Indiana Daily Student,* 3 July 2000. Available on-line:

<www.idsnews.com/news/2000.07.03/campus/2000.07.03.transfer.html>
(accessed 22 April 2001).

15. Ibid.

16. Procedures for Review of Student Conduct, Section F, Sanctions, Bing-
    hamton University of the State University of New York, 2000. Available
    on-line: <www.binghamton.edu/home/student/shandbk2000/
    conduct.html> (accessed 22 April 2001).

17. Nina Bernstein, "Behind Some Fraternity Walls, Brothers in Crime," *New
    York Times,* 6 May 1996.

18. Bradley M. Henry, interview with author, 10 January 2001.

19. Bernstein, "Behind Some Fraternity Walls, Brothers in Crime."

20. Heather Karjane, interview with author, 12 January 2001.

21. "Quality of Campus Justice Varies Widely—Rules: Most Colleges
    Surveyed Use Secretive Panels to Handle Student Misdeeds. Results
    Suffer," *Los Angeles Times,* 10 May 2000, special to the *Times,* sec. A, p. 3.

22. Michelle A. Goldfarb, interview with author, 5 June 2000.

23. "Quality of Campus Justice."

24. Ibid.

25. Ibid.

26. Security on Campus, "Campus Safety."

CHAPTER 8: WHO'S RESPONSIBLE?

1. Robert D. Bickel and Peter F. Lake, *The Rights and Responsibilities of the
   Modern University: Who Assumes the Risks of College Life?* (Durham, N.C.:
   Carolina Academic Press, 1999), 3.

2. See *Griego* v. *Hogan,* 71 N.M. 280, 377 P.2d 953, 955; *Black's Law Dictionary*
   787 (6th ed., 1990).

3. *Knoll* v. *University of Nebraska,* 258 Neb. 1, 601 N.W.2d 757 (29 Oct 1999).

4. *Coghlan* v. *Beta Theta Pi Fraternity,* 987 P.2d 300 (1999).

5. Bickel and Lake, *The Rights and Responsibilities of the Modern University.*

6. Peter F. Lake, interview with author, 6 February 2001.

7. Ibid.

8. Ethan Bronner, "In a Revolution of Rules, Campuses Go Full Circle,"
   New York Times, 3 March 1999.

9. Ibid.

10. Graham B. Spanier cited in Ethan Bronner, "In a Revolution of Rules,
    Campuses Go Full Circle," *New York Times,* 3 March 1999; Graham B.
    Spanier, interview with author, 5 October 1999.

11. Bronner, "In a Revolution of Rules."

CHAPTER 9: YOUR HEAD AND WHAT'S AHEAD

1. Elizabeth Marks, interview with author, 18 December 2000.
2. Barbara Rosen, interview with author, 9 December 2000.
3. Ibid.
4. Ibid.
5. College Parents of America, See <www.collegeparents.org>.
6. Rosen, interview with author.
7. Michael Berg, "The Parent Trap—Spending a Summer at Home with the Parents Can Be Enough to Drive Anyone Nuts." Available on-line: <www.Student.Com/article/summerathome> (accessed 21 February 2001).
8. See "What's Ahead?" *Parents Guide* (Ithaca, N.Y.: New Students Program, Office of the Dean of Students, Cornell University, 2001).
9. Pat McCoy, the Counseling Center, New Mexico State University, 13 June 1997. Available on-line: <www.nmsu.edu/~counsel/parentchild.html> (accessed 22 April 2001). Reprinted with the permission of McCoy and New Mexico State University, Las Cruces, N.M. McCoy's piece originally appeared in *The Round Up*, New Mexico State University's newspaper.

CHAPTER 10: RESOURCES FOR PARENTS

1. Leo Reisberg, "The Best Colleges That Sent in a Check—Some Guidebooks, without Telling Readers, Let Institutions Pay to Provide Information," *Chronicle of Higher Education*, 2 June 2000.
2. Ibid.
3. Ibid.

Index

■   ■   ■

About the Author

Joel Epstein is the former director of special projects and senior attorney for the U.S. Department of Education's Higher Education Center for Alcohol and Other Drug Prevention. He is currently a senior associate in the Health and Human Development Programs division at the Education Development Center in Newton, Massachusetts. A frequent speaker and media commentator on student life and college parent issues, Joel also consults to colleges, schools, Greek organizations, and attorneys on policy and legal compliance, student safety, risk management, and media relations.

Joel's prior writing has covered topics ranging from the law of student safety to residential crime prevention, criminal prosecution, and environmental protection. A graduate of the University of Michigan and the Benjamin N. Cardozo School of Law, Joel lives in the Boston area with his wife and three children.

HAZELDEN PUBLISHING AND EDUCATIONAL SERVICES
is a division of the Hazelden Foundation, a not-for-profit organization. Since 1949, Hazelden has been a leader in promoting the dignity and treatment of people afflicted with the disease of chemical dependency.

The mission of the foundation is to improve the quality of life for individuals, families, and communities by providing a national continuum of information, education, and recovery services that are widely accessible; to advance the field through research and training; and to improve our quality and effectiveness through continuous improvement and innovation.

Stemming from that, the mission of this division is to provide quality information and support to people wherever they may be in their personal journey—from education and early intervention, through treatment and recovery, to personal and spiritual growth.

Although our treatment programs do not necessarily use everything Hazelden publishes, our bibliotherapeutic materials support our mission and the Twelve Step philosophy upon which it is based. We encourage your comments and feedback.

The headquarters of the Hazelden Foundation are in Center City, Minnesota. Additional treatment facilities are located in Chicago, Illinois; New York, New York; Plymouth, Minnesota; St. Paul, Minnesota; and West Palm Beach, Florida. At these sites, we provide a continuum of care for men and women of all ages. Our Plymouth facility is designed specifically for youth and families.

For more information on Hazelden, please call **1-800-257-7800**. Or you may access our World Wide Web site on the Internet at **www.hazelden.org**.